BASICS

SIMPLE EASY TO FOLLOW RECIPES WITH STEP-BY-STEP PHOTOS

TRIPLE TESTED

PUBLISHED IN 2016 BY BOUNTY BOOKS BASED ON MATERIALS
LICENSED TO IT BY BAUER MEDIA BOOKS, AUSTRALIA.

BAUER MEDIA BOOKS ARE PUBLISHED BY
BAUER MEDIA PTY LIMITED
54 PARK ST, SYDNEY; GPO BOX 4088,
SYDNEY, NSW 2001 AUSTRALIA
PHONE +61 2 9282 8618; FAX +61 2 9126 3702
WWW.AWWCOOKBOOKS.COM.AU

PUBLISHER
JO RUNCIMAN

EDITORIAL & FOOD DIRECTOR
PAMELA CLARK

DIRECTOR OF SALES, MARKETING & RIGHTS
BRIAN CEARNES

CREATIVE DIRECTOR & DESIGNER
HANNAH BLACKMORE

SENIOR EDITOR
STEPHANIE KISTNER

FOOD EDITORS
SOPHIA YOUNG, ALEXANDRA ELLIOTT

OPERATIONS MANAGER
DAVID SCOTTO

PRINTED IN CHINA
BY LEO PAPER PRODUCTS LTD

PUBLISHED AND DISTRIBUTED IN THE
UNITED KINGDOM BY BOUNTY BOOKS,
A DIVISION OF OCTOPUS PUBLISHING GROUP LTD
CARMELITE HOUSE
50 VICTORIA EMBANKMENT
LONDON, EC4Y 0DZ
UNITED KINGDOM
INFO@OCTOPUS-PUBLISHING.CO.UK;
WWW.OCTOPUSBOOKS.CO.UK

INTERNATIONAL FOREIGN LANGUAGE RIGHTS
BRIAN CEARNES, BAUER MEDIA BOOKS
BCEARNES@BAUER-MEDIA.COM.AU

A CATALOGUE RECORD FOR THIS BOOK IS
AVAILABLE FROM THE BRITISH LIBRARY.

ISBN: 978-0-75373-094-2

© BAUER MEDIA PTY LTD 2016

ABN 18 053 273 546

BASICS

SIMPLE EASY TO FOLLOW RECIPES WITH STEP-BY-STEP PHOTOS

BB **Bounty**
Books

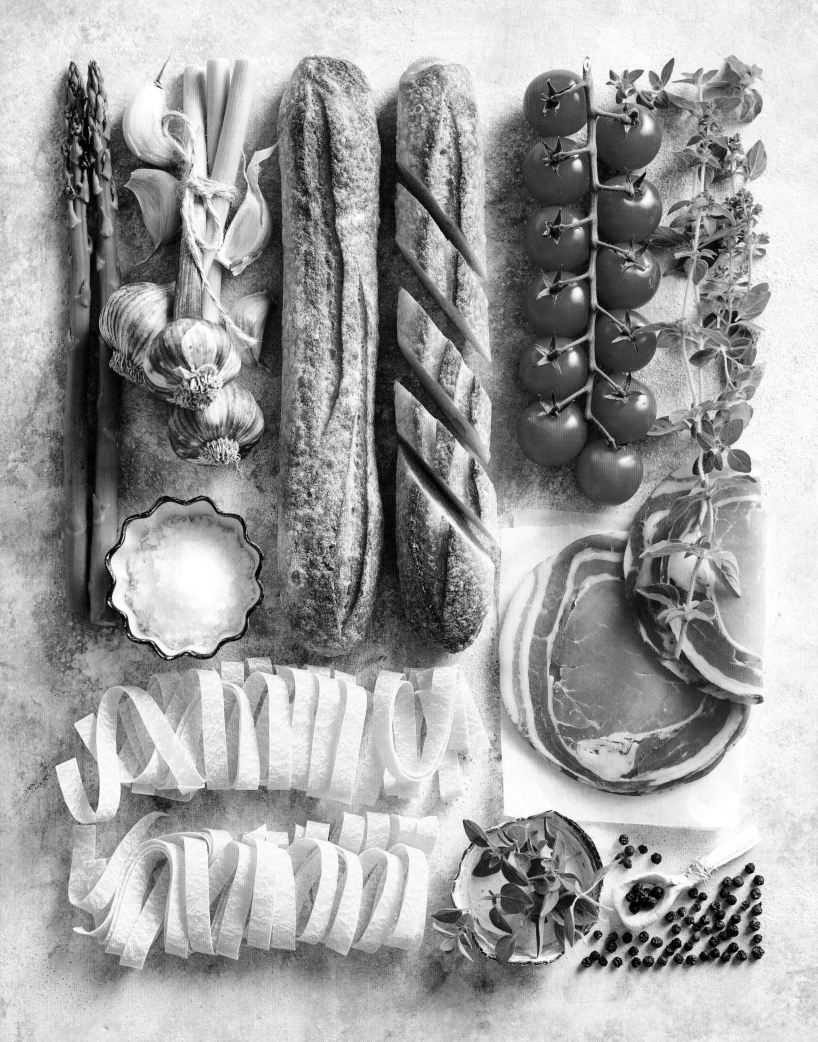

CONTENTS

KITCHEN ESSENTIALS

When setting up your kitchen, start with utensils you'll use all the time, and fill the pantry with a range of standby items.

1 Slotted spoon
2 Utility knife
3 Wooden spoon
4 Pastry brush
5 Small whisk
6 Balloon whisk
7 & 8 Measuring cups
9 Measuring spoon
10 Egg whisk
11 Garlic crusher
12 Wooden citrus reamer (juicer)
13 Enamel frying pan

PANTRY BASICS

Essential canned foods to have on standby are: tomatoes, tuna, beans and anchovies. Then stock up on a good range of pastas, rice, pulse and grains. To keep fresh, transfer items to airtight containers; date and label. Only buy spices in small quantities to ensure their freshness. Useful spices are fennel seeds with its anise-like flavour (use in Italian dishes, with Mediterranean vegetables, seafood and lamb) warm earthy cumin and coriander with it's floral note. Spice mixes such as dukkah, Moroccan seasoning or ras el hanout and garam marsala are a great way to use one ingredient and add a lot of flavour. For herbs, fresh is always best. It's also helpful to have a range of oils (extra virgin olive oil, vegetable oil and coconut oil), vinegars (red and white wine, rice wine and balsamic) and Asian sauces (oyster, soy sauce, kecap manis, fish sauce and hoisin) on hand to use as the flavour building blocks of a recipe. Once open, transfer them to the fridge. Potatoes, onions and garlic should be stored out of the fridge in a cool, dark, dry place. Remove any plastic packaging, place in a basket or crate, or similar container where air can circulate.

FRIDGE BASICS

Your fridge should be used to turn over ingredients quite quickly. Delicate vegetables are best stored in the crisper, where the slightly lower temperature will insulate them from fridge burn. Chopped and minced meats should be used within a couple of days, as should seafood. Large cuts of meat, and those on the bone will last longer, as will anything cryovaced; refer to use-by-dates. Cooked foods should be eaten within a couple of days.

FROZEN BASICS

Make sure that everything you freeze is clearly identifiable with a name and date. To avoid freezer burn, eliminate air from bags or place in airtight containers. As a guide, minced meat, chops and steaks will keep frozen for up to 3 months. Large roasts and whole chicken, will keep for up to 6 months. White fish fillets will keep for up to 6 months and oily fish and shell fish up to 2 months. Cooked homemade food should be cooled slightly, then place into the fridge to cool completely.

EGGS

BOILED EGGS

PREP + COOK TIME 10 MINUTES **MAKES** 4

Place 4 room temperature eggs in a small saucepan with enough cold water to just cover the eggs. Cover with the lid. Bring the water to the boil over high heat, then remove the lid. Boil eggs until yolks are as soft or as firm as you like (see side panel at right, for cooking times). Remove eggs from water. Serve immediately with salt, pepper and buttered toast fingers. For medium- or hard-boiled eggs, cool under cold running water. Roll eggs on a work surface to crack the shell; peel.

tip To centralise each yolk, which looks good if you are halving them for a salad, stir the eggs continuously with a wooden spoon over high heat until the water boils.

COOKING TIMES

Choose a cooking time to cook your eggs to perfection.

3 minutes for soft-boiled (set white, runny yolk)

4 minutes for medium-boiled (set white, set yolk)

5 minutes for hard-boiled (set white, set yolk)

FRIED EGGS

PREP + COOK TIME 8 MINUTES **SERVES** 1

Break a room temperature egg into a small bowl or saucer. Melt about 20g (¾oz) butter per egg in a small non-stick frying pan over medium heat, then gently slide the egg into the centre of the pan. (If cooking more than 1 egg at a time, use a larger pan so all eggs fit to cook at once or in two batches.) Fry the egg gently, basting the yolk occasionally with the butter, until cooked to your liking (see side panel at left, for cooking styles). Remove the cooked egg from the pan with an egg slide, allowing excess butter to drain off the egg before serving on buttered toast, seasoned with salt and pepper, and with tomato chutney.

COOKING STYLES

Sunny-side up The white is firm and the yolk is cooked to your liking. For crisp edges on the whites, start with a high heat for 30 seconds then reduce to medium heat.

Over easy If you also like the yolk to be set, turn the egg over and cook until just set.

11

POACHED EGGS

PREP + COOK TIME 5 MINUTES **MAKES** 4

2 teaspoons white vinegar • 4 fresh free-range eggs

Half-fill a large shallow frying pan with water; add vinegar.
Bring to the boil. Break 1 egg into a small bowl or cup.
Swirl the boiling water with a whisk to create a whirlpool,
then slide the egg into the pan. Repeat with remaining eggs.
When all the eggs are in the pan, allow the water to return
to the boil. Cover the pan, then turn off the heat; stand for
4 minutes or until a light film of egg white sets over the yolks.
Remove eggs with a slotted spoon; drain on paper towel.

Use free-range, very fresh, eggs as they will keep their shape better in the water. To test for freshness, place eggs in a bowl of water – a fresh egg will lie on the bottom, while a stale egg with float, big end up.

Make a whirlpool in a large shallow saucepan or frying pan of boiling water using a whisk. Putting the eggs into the whirlpool will help to keep the whites in a neat shape.

Break one egg into a small bowl or cup then gently slide it into the whirlpool. Add remaining eggs, one at a time. When all the eggs are in the pan, allow the water to return to the boil.

Using a slotted spoon, carefully remove the eggs, one at a time, onto a plate lined with paper towel to drain; cover to keep them warm. Trim the whites of any ragged edges with scissors.

BACON & EGG MUFFIN

PREP + COOK TIME 25 MINUTES **SERVES** 4

While we've poached the eggs in this recipe, you could fry the eggs (see page 11) instead. For more information on poaching eggs, see pages 12 & 13.

½ cup (150g) whole-egg mayonnaise

½ clove garlic, crushed

2 tablespoons micro basil, optional (see tips)

8 rindless bacon slices (500g)

8 free-range eggs (see tips)

4 english muffins (260g)

50g (1½ ounces) baby spinach leaves

1 Combine mayonnaise, garlic and half the micro basil in a small bowl; season to taste.
2 Cook bacon in a large frying pan over medium-high heat until crisp. Drain on paper towel. Cover to keep warm.
3 For poached eggs, half-fill a large shallow frying pan with water; add vinegar. Bring to the boil. Break 1 egg into a small bowl or cup. Swirl the boiling water with a whisk to create a whirlpool, then slide the egg into the pan. Repeat with 3 more eggs. Return to the boil. Cover the pan, then turn off the heat; stand for 4 minutes or until a light film of egg white sets over the yolks. Remove eggs with a slotted spoon; drain on paper towel. Repeat with remaining eggs.
4 Meanwhile, preheat grill (broiler). Split muffins in half; place under grill until toasted.
5 Spread aïoli on toasted muffins; top with bacon, eggs and remaining basil. Season. Serve with spinach.

tips Garlic mayonnaise is also known as aïoli. You can use regular chopped basil, dill or chives in the garlic mayonnaise (aïoli) instead of half the micro basil, if you like. Use free-range, very fresh eggs for poaching as they will keep their shape better.

SCRAMBLED EGGS

PREP + COOK TIME 20 MINUTES **SERVES** 4

8 eggs • ½ cup (125ml) pouring cream •
30g (1 ounce) butter

Lightly whisk eggs and cream in a medium bowl.
Heat butter in a large frying pan over medium heat.
Add egg mixture, wait a few seconds, then use a wide
spatula to gently scrape the set egg mixture along the base
of the pan. Remove from heat when eggs are still creamy
and barely set. Serve immediately, with toast, if you like.

SCRAMBLED EGGS · TOPPINGS

SMOKED SALMON

Serve scrambled eggs on toast topped with 100g (3oz) torn smoked salmon slices and 1 tablespoon chopped dill sprigs. Serve with lemon wedges.

HERBS

Finely chop 1 tablespoon each fresh chives, flat-leaf parsley and basil. Serve scrambled eggs on toast, topped with herbs.

BACON

Cook 4 chopped trimmed bacon slices in a small frying pan until browned; drain on paper towel. Serve scrambled eggs on toast topped with bacon and 1 cup picked watercress sprigs.

PERSIAN FETTA & THYME

Serve scrambled eggs on toast topped with 100g (3oz) drained, crumbled persian fetta or soft goat's cheese, 2 teaspoons fresh thyme and 1 teaspoon finely grated lemon rind.

QUICHE LORRAINE

PREP + COOK TIME 1 HOUR 30 MINUTES (+ REFRIGERATION) **SERVES** 6

2 teaspoons olive oil

1 medium onion (150g), chopped finely

3 rindless bacon slices (195g), chopped finely

3 eggs

300ml pouring cream

½ cup (125ml) milk

¾ cup (120g) coarsely grated gruyère cheese

pastry

1¾ cups (260g) plain (all-purpose) flour

150g (4½ ounces) cold butter, chopped coarsely

1 egg yolk

2 teaspoons lemon juice

1 tablespoon iced water

1 Make pastry.

2 Preheat oven to 200°C/400°F.

3 Roll pastry between sheets of baking paper until large enough to line a 25cm (10-inch) round, 3.5cm (1½-inch) deep, loose-based fluted tart tin. Lift pastry into tin; gently press pastry into the base and side. Trim edge. Place tin on oven tray. Line pastry case with baking paper; fill with dried beans or rice. Bake for 10 minutes. Remove paper and beans; bake for a further 10 minutes or until golden. Cool.

4 Reduce oven to 180°C/350°F.

5 Heat oil in a small frying pan over medium heat; cook onion and bacon, stirring, for 8 minutes or until onion is soft. Drain on paper towel. Cool. Sprinkle bacon mixture on pastry case.

6 Whisk eggs in a medium bowl; whisk in cream, milk and cheese. Pour mixture into pastry case.

7 Bake quiche for 35 minutes or until filling is set (see tips). Leave in tin for 5 minutes before removing from tin.

pastry Sift flour into a medium bowl; rub in butter. Add egg yolk, juice and enough of the water to make ingredients cling together. Knead gently on a floured surface until smooth. Cover; refrigerate 30 minutes.

tips A perfect quiche should be slightly soft to touch at the centre as it will continue to set a little more on standing. To test if it's cooked, insert a thin-bladed knife into the centre; if the knife comes out clean, the quiche is cooked. You can use grated cheddar instead of gruyère, if you prefer.

BASIC OMELETTE

PREP + COOK TIME 10 MINUTES **SERVES** 4

12 eggs • ⅓ cup (80ml) water • 40g (1½ ounces) butter

Beat eggs and water in a large bowl with a fork until combined. Season. Heat a quarter of the butter in a small frying pan over medium heat. When the butter is foaming, add a quarter of the egg mixture. Using a wide spatula, gently push the set egg mixture toward the centre of pan; tilt the pan, allowing the uncooked egg mixture to run onto the base of the pan. Repeat about four times around the pan, until the egg is just set. Fold one side of the omelette over using the spatula. Slide onto a plate. Repeat, wiping out pan with paper towel before each addition, to make a total of 4 omelettes.

SAUTEED MUSHROOMS & HERBS

Heat 30g (1oz) butter in a large frying pan over high heat; cook 250g (8oz) baby button mushrooms or sliced mushrooms, stirring, for 5 minutes or until browned. Season. Divide mushrooms and 2 tablespoons each chopped fresh flat-leaf parsley and chives between omelettes.

SMOKED SALMON, DILL & CAPERS

Divide 100g (3oz) smoked salmon or ocean trout slices, 2 tablespoons fresh dill sprigs, 2 teaspoons drained baby capers and a few thin slices red onion between omelettes. Season omelettes with salt and freshly ground black pepper.

TOMATO & PERSIAN FETTA

Remove seeds from 2 vine-ripened tomatoes (see Vegetable Techniques page 198), then finely dice. Divide tomatoes, 100g (3oz) drained, crumbled persian fetta and 1 tablespoon fresh oregano leaves between omelettes.

BACON & SPINACH

Thinly slice 4 rindless slices bacon; cook in a small frying pan over high heat until browned, drain on paper towel. Divide bacon and 100g (3oz) baby spinach leaves between omelettes; season with ground black pepper.

ASPARAGUS & FETTA FRITTATA

PREP + COOK TIME 35 MINUTES (+ COOLING) **SERVES** 4

A frittata is great for a brunch, casual lunch or a picnic, as it can be served cold or at room temperature.

170g (5½ ounces) asparagus, trimmed

8 eggs

½ cup (125ml) pouring cream

½ cup lightly packed fresh mint leaves, torn

2 small zucchini (180g), sliced thinly lengthways (see tip)

1 cup (120g) frozen peas, thawed

150g (4½ ounces) fetta, crumbled

1 Preheat oven to 180°C/350°F. Oil a 20cm x 30cm (8-inch x 12-inch) rectangular pan; line base with baking paper, extending the paper 5cm (2 inches) over the long sides.

2 Cook asparagus in a small saucepan of boiling water for 1 minute. Drain immediately. Transfer asparagus to a bowl of iced water until cold. Drain well; pat dry with paper towel.

3 Whisk eggs and cream in a large jug until combined. Add mint; season.

4 Place half of each vegetable and half the fetta in the pan; pour over half the egg mixture.

5 Bake frittata for 10 minutes. Add remaining egg mixture, vegetables and fetta; bake for a further 15 minutes or until set. Cool before cutting into slices. Serve with lemon wedges and char-grilled bread, if you like.

tip If you have one, use a mandoline or V-slicer to quickly and easily cut the zucchini into thin slices (see General Techniques page 228).

COOKING NOTES

You can start cooking this frittata in a non-stick ovenproof frying pan on the stove top and finish it under the grill (broiler). The frittata can be eaten warm or at room temperature. Cooled frittata can be stored, covered, in the fridge for up to 2 days.

BUTTERMILK PANCAKES

PREP + COOK TIME 30 MINUTES **SERVES** 4

2 eggs • 1½ cups (375ml) buttermilk •
¼ cup (55g) caster (superfine) sugar • 2 cups (300g) self-raising flour •
½ teaspoon bicarbonate of (baking) soda • 40g (1½ ounces) butter

Whisk eggs, buttermilk, sugar and combined sifted flour and soda
in a medium bowl until smooth. Melt 1 teaspoon of the butter in a
medium frying pan. Pour ⅓-cups of batter into pan; cook pancakes
for 2 minutes or until bubbles appear on the surface. Turn; cook other
side until browned. Remove from pan. Repeat to make a total of
8 pancakes. Serve with maple syrup or one of the toppings opposite.

BACON & MAPLE SYRUP

Cook 4 rindless bacon slices (260g) in a small frying pan over medium heat until crisp; drain on paper towel. Serve pancakes topped with bacon and ¾ cup pure maple syrup.

VANILLA & RED BERRIES

Stir 1 teaspoon vanilla bean paste or extract into pancake batter before cooking. Serve pancakes topped with 250g (8oz) halved strawberries and 200g (6½oz) raspberries, dusted with icing sugar.

HONEYCOMB BUTTER

Beat 125g (4oz) softened butter with an electric mixer until pale. Stir in ⅓ cup chopped honeycomb confectionery. Serve pancakes topped with honeycomb butter, orange rind strips and nutmeg.

WALNUTS, LEMON & SUGAR

Serve pancakes topped with 100g (3oz) coarsely chopped roasted walnuts, 2 tablespoons caster (superfine) sugar, micro mint or small fresh mint leaves and lemon wedges.

BLUEBERRIES & CINNAMON SUGAR

Stir ½ cup blueberries into pancake batter before cooking. Serve pancakes topped with extra blueberries, 2 tablespoons cinnamon sugar and maple syrup.

BANANA & SALTED CARAMEL

Melt 100g (3oz) butter, ½ cup firmly packed brown sugar, ½ cup pouring cream and ¼ teaspoon sea salt in a small saucepan; simmer for 2 minutes. Serve pancakes topped with sliced banana and sauce.

COCONUT, YOGHURT & LIME

Combine ½ cup each coconut flakes and roasted macadamias. Toss 2 sliced limes with 2 tablespoons caster (superfine) sugar. Serve pancakes with yoghurt, coconut mixture, limes and micro herbs.

DOUBLE CHOCOLATE

Stir ½ cup dark choc bits into pancake batter before cooking. Melt 100g (3oz) dark choc bits with ½ cup pouring cream in a saucepan until smooth. Serve pancakes topped with ice-cream and sauce.

SEEDS, FIGS & HONEY

Stir 1 tablespoon each pepitas (pumpkin seeds), sesame seeds and sunflower seeds into pancake batter before cooking. Serve pancakes topped with greek-style yoghurt, halved fresh figs and honey.

MEAT

CHAR-GRILLING OR BARBECUING

Preheat a char-grill pan or barbecue on high heat for 5 minutes before adding the meat. Brush the meat to be cooked with oil just before cooking, rather than oiling the char-grill pan or barbecue. Season the meat with a little salt if not using a marinade. Cook the first side until browned to your liking. When the blood has risen to the surface, turn the meat and cook on the second side until done as desired. (For cross-hatch char marks, turn the meat 45 degrees halfway through the cooking time on one side.) Transfer cooked meat to a plate and cover loosely with foil; leave the meat to rest for 5 minutes before serving.

STIR-FRYING

Meat is composed of small and large muscle fibres. The "grain" of the meat is the direction in which these fibres run. Cutting across the grain severs these fibres, making the meat more tender, while thinly slicing it makes it quick cooking for stir-frying. To achieve thin slices of meat, partially freeze it (or partially thaw it if it is already frozen). When the meat is firm you will find it is easier to slice thinly. Allow it to thaw for a few minutes at room temperature before stir-frying. Stir-fry meat in small batches, so as not to over crowd the wok, which cools the wok down too much and stews the meat, rather than browns it.

ROASTING

For a more even cooking time and to keep the meat in neat shape, tie roasts such as eye fillet, scotch fillet, standing rib roast, lamb or pork loin or boneless rolled roasts with string. Use kitchen string and tie the meat at 2cm (¾-inch) intervals. Roasting is best done in a roasting pan made of metal which is a much better conductor of heat, than baking dishes which are made from glass or ceramic (these transfer heat poorly and can slow the cooking time and decrease browning). After resting the meat at the end of cooking time, don't forget to remove the string before carving.

SLOW COOKING

When browning or searing pieces of meat for slow cooking, cook the meat in small batches. It's important to keep the heat high and the pan hot.

If you cook too many pieces at a time, they'll release a lot of juices and stew rather than brown.

Also, don't cut the pieces of meat too small, unless the recipe specifies. It's better to cook in larger chunks 5cm (2 inches) that can be broken up when tender. The best meats for slow cooking are secondary cuts – these cuts contain lots of gelatinous connective tissues, which break down during the long cooking time and help to keep the meat moist. Lean prime cuts will simply become dry during long slow cooking.

PERFECT STEAK

Preheat a heavy-based frying pan, char-grill pan or barbecue over a high heat until hot. Brush or rub steaks with olive oil. Season with a little salt and freshly ground black pepper. Cook steaks over high heat to your liking, following instructions below. Turn steaks once using tongs, not a fork. To test if steak is ready, use the blunt end of the tongs to press the meat in the thickest part. Remove steak from the heat, cover with foil and rest for 5 minutes; this will make the steak more tender. Serve steak with pan juices and wholegrain mustard or one of the classic sauces, opposite.

WELL DONE Cook on one side until moisture is pooling on top. Cook on second side until moisture is pooling on top. Reduce heat slightly; cook until steak feels very firm when pressed.

MEDIUM Cook on one side until moisture is pooling on top. Cook on second side until surface moisture is visible. Cook until steak feels springy when pressed with tongs.

RARE Cook for a few minutes per side, depending on thickness. Cook until steak feels very soft when pressed with tongs.

PEPPER SAUCE

Season steak with plenty of coarsely ground black pepper. Pan-fry steak, then remove from pan. Add 1 crushed clove garlic to same pan; stir for 1 minute. Stir in 1 tablespoon drained canned green peppercorns, crushed lightly, 1 teaspoon dijon mustard, ¾ cup beef stock and ¾ cup pouring cream; simmer, uncovered, until thickened. Serve with steak.

CHIMICHURRI

In a small food processor, process 1 tablespoon red wine vinegar, ½ cup extra virgin olive oil, 2 halved cloves garlic, ½ teaspoon dried chilli flakes, 1 teaspoon sea salt flakes, 2 cups loosely packed fresh flat-leaf parsley leaves, 1 teaspoon dried oregano and 1 tablespoon lemon juice until finely chopped. Season. Serve with pan-fried steak.

CREAMY MUSHROOM SAUCE

Pan-fry steak, then remove from pan. Melt 40g (1½oz) butter in same pan over medium-high heat; cook 400g (12½oz) sliced button mushrooms, stirring occasionally, until browned. Add 1 crushed clove garlic; stir 1 minute. Stir in ¾ cup beef stock and ¾ cup pouring cream; simmer until thickened slightly. Stir in 2 tablespoons chopped fresh flat-leaf parsley. Serve with steak.

RED WINE & SHALLOT SAUCE

Pan-fry steak, then remove from pan. Melt 20g (¾oz) butter in same pan over medium heat; cook 6 peeled and halved shallots, stirring occasionally, until soft. Stir in ½ cup red wine; simmer until reduced by half. Stir in 1 cup beef stock and 1 teaspoon worcestershire sauce; simmer until thickened slightly. Serve with steak.

STICKY SOY & LIME RIBS

PREP + COOK TIME 2 HOURS (+ REFRIGERATION) **SERVES** 2

1kg (2 pounds) american-style pork spare ribs, cut into pieces

1 cup (320g) plum jam

1 cup (250ml) water

2 tablespoons finely grated lime rind

2 tablespoons lime juice

2 tablespoons soy sauce

2 teaspoons garlic powder

2 teaspoons onion powder

1 teaspoon dried chilli flakes

1 teaspoon ground cumin

coriander sprigs and lime wedges, to serve

1 Place ribs in a large saucepan with enough cold water to cover. Cover; bring to the boil. Reduce heat to low; skim away impurities from the surface. Simmer, covered, for 30 minutes. Drain.

2 Combine remaining ingredients in a large bowl, add ribs; turn to coat. Cover; refrigerate for at least 2 hours or overnight, turning occasionally.

3 Preheat oven to 200°C/400°F.

4 Place ribs and marinade in a large baking-paper-lined dish; season. Roast for 1 hour, turning and brushing every 15 minutes with pan juices. Cut into individual ribs, serve topped with coriander and lime wedges.

tips You will need about 2 limes for the juice needed. To save on cleaning, line the dishes with a layer of foil or use disposable foil baking dishes.

MOROCCAN LAMB CUTLETS WITH COUSCOUS SALAD

PREP + COOK TIME 30 MINUTES **SERVES** 4

2 teaspoons ras el hanout

⅓ cup (80ml) olive oil

12 french-trimmed lamb cutlets (600g)

1 medium green capsicum (bell pepper) (200g)

1 medium yellow capsicum (bell pepper) (200g)

1 medium red capsicum (bell pepper) (200g)

2 cups (500ml) water

30g (1 ounce) butter

1 teaspoon sea salt flakes

2 cups (400g) couscous

200g (6½ ounces) hummus

¼ cup torn fresh flat-leaf parsley leaves

1 medium lemon (140g), rind cut into strips, curled (see General Techniques page 228)

1 Preheat grill (broiler).

2 Combine ras el hanout and half the oil in a large bowl; add lamb, turn to coat in mixture.

3 Quarter capsicums; discard seeds and membrane. Place, skin-side up, on a foil-lined oven tray; drizzle with remaining oil. Place under hot grill for 15 minutes or until skin blisters and blackens. Cover capsicum with plastic wrap or paper, leave 5 minutes; peel away skin, then slice thinly.

4 Meanwhile, bring the water, butter and salt to the boil in a medium saucepan; stir in couscous. Remove pan from heat; cover, stand for 5 minutes. Fluff couscous with a fork.

5 Spoon hummus into a small serving bowl; sprinkle with a little extra ras el hanout.

6 Place couscous and capsicum in a large bowl with parsley and rind; toss gently to combine.

7 Cook lamb on a heated oiled char-grill plate (or grill or barbecue) for 4 minutes each side or until cooked as desired. Serve lamb with couscous salad and hummus.

tips You can use 8 lamb loin chops (800g) instead of the cutlets, if you prefer. Store-bought char-grilled capsicum could be used.

serving suggestion Serve with char-grilled lemon halves. Place lemon halves, cut-side down, on a heated char-grill pan for 2 minutes.

FIVE-SPICE PORK CUTLETS WITH PLUM SAUCE

PREP + COOK TIME 20 MINUTES **SERVES** 4

4 pork cutlets (940g)

1 tablespoon chinese five spice powder

2 tablespoons peanut oil

1 bunch choy sum (400g)

450g (14½ ounces) packaged microwave white rice

1 fresh long red chilli, sliced thinly

fresh coriander (cilantro) leaves, to serve

plum sauce

⅓ cup (75g) firmly packed brown sugar

½ cup (125ml) water

6 drained canned whole plums (250g)

1 tablespoon chinese cooking wine (shao hsing)

1 cinnamon stick

2 star anise

2 tablespoons fish sauce

2 teaspoons malt vinegar

1 Combine pork, five spice and oil in a large bowl; season.

2 Heat a large frying pan over medium-high heat; cook pork for 3 minutes each side or until cooked through. Remove from pan, cover; rest for 5 minutes.

3 Meanwhile, make plum sauce.

4 Microwave choy sum until just wilted.

5 Heat rice according to directions on packet.

6 Serve pork on rice and choy sum, topped with chilli and coriander; drizzle with plum sauce.

plum sauce Stir sugar and the water in a medium saucepan over low heat until sugar dissolves. Discard stones from plums; add plums to pan with wine, cinnamon and star anise. Bring to the boil. Reduce heat; simmer, covered, for 6 minutes or until plums are pulpy. Remove and discard cinnamon stick. Stir in fish sauce and vinegar; season to taste.

tip You can use fresh plums when in season.

COOKING NOTES

It's not necessary to add oil to a frying pan when cooking bacon as the fat renders in the hot pan, creating its own frying medium. To keep sausages juicy, don't pierce them during cooking. Use a moderate heat, turning them frequently, until browned all over. To test if cooked, pierce one sausage on the side; if juices are clear, it's cooked.

BEEF SAUSAGES & BEER ONIONS WITH PEA & BACON MASH

PREP + COOK TIME 25 MINUTES **SERVES** 4

3 rindless bacon slices (200g), chopped

2 tablespoons olive oil

3 medium onions (450g), sliced thickly

¼ cup (55g) firmly packed brown sugar

330ml bottle beer

1 tablespoon wholegrain mustard

3 sprigs fresh thyme

1kg (2 pounds) potatoes, peeled, quartered

1 cup (250ml) milk, warmed

40g (1½ ounces) butter

1 cup (120g) frozen peas

8 thick beef sausages (640g) (see tip)

1 Heat a large frying pan over medium heat; cook bacon, stirring, until browned and crisp. Drain on paper towel.

2 Heat oil in same pan over medium heat, add onions and a pinch of salt; cook, covered, for 5 minutes or until softened. Turn onions. Add sugar, beer, mustard and thyme; boil for 5 minutes or until liquid is reduced by half. Remove from pan; cover to keep warm.

3 Meanwhile, boil or steam potatoes until soft; drain. Mash potatoes with milk and butter; season to taste. Boil, steam or microwave peas until just tender; drain. Stir peas and bacon through mash; keep warm, covered, over low heat.

4 Cook sausages in same cleaned frying pan, over medium heat, turning occasionally with tongs, until sausages are browned all over and cooked through.

5 Serve sausages and onions with mash.

tip There are many plain and flavoured sausages available using beef, lamb, pork and chicken. Use your favourite flavour and thickness.

BASIC MINCE

PREP + COOK TIME 15 MINUTES **SERVES** 6

2 slices white bread (90g) • ⅓ cup (80ml) milk •
1 tablespoon olive oil • 1 medium brown onion (150g),
chopped finely • 2 cloves garlic, crushed • 1 medium carrot
(120g), grated finely • 1kg (2 pounds) minced (ground) beef •
¼ cup chopped fresh flat-leaf parsley • 1 egg •
2 tablespoons tomato paste

Place bread and milk in a large bowl; stand 10 minutes.
Heat oil in a small frying pan over medium heat; cook onion
and garlic, stirring, for 5 minutes or until softened. Add
onion mixture to bread mixture with remaining ingredients;
season well. Combine ingredients well using your hands.

MEATLOAF

Preheat oven to 200°C/400°F. Line a large oven tray with baking paper.
Shape Basic Mince (left) into a 30cm (12-in) log in centre of paper.
Cover mixture with 100g (3oz) pancetta slices, slightly overlapping.
Brush with ¼ cup barbecue sauce combined with 1 tablespoon brown sugar.
Bake meatloaf for 45 minutes or until cooked through.

MEATBALLS

Shape 1½ tablespoons of Basic Mince (left) into balls. Heat 1 tablespoon
olive oil in a large deep frying pan; cook balls, in batches, until browned.
Remove from pan. Add 700g (1½lbs) tomato passata and 1 cup chicken stock
to pan; bring to the boil. Return meatballs to pan. Reduce heat; simmer,
5 minutes or until cooked. Serve with parmesan and basil leaves.

KOFTA

Make a half quantity of Basic Mince (left), adding 1 tablespoon ground
cumin, 2 teaspoons ground allspice and 1 tablespoon chopped fresh mint.
Divide mix into 18 portions and mould around skewers. Cook kofta, in
batches, on heated oiled grill plate or barbecue until cooked through.
Serve with pitta, yoghurt and lemon wedges.

HAMBURGERS

Shape Basic Mince (left) into 6 patties. Refrigerate for 15 minutes.
Cook patties in a large oiled frying pan or barbecue plate over medium-high
heat for 5 minutes each side or until cooked through. Halve and toast
4 burger buns. Sandwich buns with mayonnaise, lettuce, sliced tomato,
beef patties and sliced cheddar. Serve with pickles.

SAUSAGE ROLLS

PREP + COOK TIME 35 MINUTES **MAKES** 72

1 medium onion (150g), chopped finely

½ cup (35g) stale breadcrumbs (see tips)

500g (1 pound) sausage mince

500g (1 pound) minced (ground) beef

1 egg

1 tablespoon tomato paste

1 tablespoon barbecue sauce

2 tablespoons finely chopped fresh flat-leaf parsley

6 sheets puff pastry

1 egg, extra, beaten lightly

2 tablespoons sesame seeds

1 Preheat oven to 220°C/425°F. Line oven trays with baking paper.

2 Combine onion, breadcrumbs, sausage mince and beef, egg, paste, sauce and parsley in a large bowl.

3 Cut pastry sheets in half lengthways. Place equal amounts of filling mixture lengthways along centre of each pastry piece (see tips); roll each pastry piece, from one wide edge, to enclose filling. Cut each roll into six pieces; place rolls, seam-side down, on trays. Brush with extra egg, sprinkle with sesame seeds.

4 Bake rolls for 25 minutes or until golden and puffed. Serve sausage rolls hot with tomato sauce (ketchup) or chutney, if you like.

tips To make stale breadcrumbs, use 2-3 day old bread and process in batches (see also General Techniques page 229). An easy way to make sure that you get an equal amount of filling mixture in each sausage roll is to pipe it down the length of the pastry, using a piping bag fitted with a 2cm (¾-inch) plain tube. Uncooked sausage rolls keep well in the freezer for up to 3 months. Allow an extra 5 minutes when baking from frozen.

RECIPE VARIATIONS

Middle-Eastern Use minced lamb in place of both minces, 2 tablespoons middle-eastern spice blend instead of barbecue sauce and coriander instead of parsley.

Pork + Fennel Use minced pork in place of both minces, add ½ teaspoon celery salt, 2 teaspoons coarsely pounded fennel seeds and chopped dill in place of parsley. Swap fennel seeds for sesame.

FLAVOUR BOOSTERS

Guacamole Mash a ripe avocado in a bowl. Stir in ¼ finely chopped red onion, 1 tablespoon lime juice, 2 tablespoons chopped fresh coriander (cilantro) and salt to taste.

Tomato salsa Combine 2 finely chopped roma (egg) tomatoes with 1 tablespoon olive oil, ¼ finely chopped red onion and Tabasco.

BEEF BURRITOS

PREP + COOK TIME 45 MINUTES **MAKES** 4

1 tablespoon olive oil

1 medium onion (150g), chopped finely

1 clove garlic, crushed

1 teaspoon ground cumin

¼ teaspoon chilli powder

500g (1 pound) minced (ground) beef

400g (12½ ounces) canned crushed tomatoes

½ cup (125ml) water

400g (12½ ounces) canned kidney beans, drained, rinsed

4 x 20cm (8-inch) flour tortillas

1 cup (120g) coarsely grated cheddar

1 teaspoon hot paprika

¼ cup fresh baby coriander (cilantro) leaves

1 Heat oil in a medium frying pan over high heat; cook onion, garlic, cumin and chilli powder, stirring, for 3 minutes or until onion has softened. Add beef; cook, stirring, until browned. Stir in tomatoes, the water and beans; simmer, uncovered, for 15 minutes or until mixture thickens. Remove from heat; season to taste.

2 Meanwhile, preheat oven to 200°C/400°F.

3 Divide warm beef filling among tortillas, roll to enclose the filling; secure with toothpicks. Place tortillas on an oiled oven tray; sprinkle with cheddar and paprika.

4 Bake burritos for 10 minutes or until heated through. Remove toothpicks; top with coriander. Serve burritos topped with guacamole and tomato salsa (see flavour boosters, page opposite).

tip Mix it up and try canned black beans instead of kidney beans and corn tortillas instead of flour tortillas.

TURKISH-STYLE PIZZA WITH MINTED YOGHURT

PREP + COOK TIME 50 MINUTES **SERVES** 4

¼ cup (60ml) olive oil

1 medium onion (150g), chopped finely

1 clove garlic, crushed

500g (1 pound) minced (ground) lamb or beef

1 teaspoon chilli flakes

2 teaspoons ground cumin

½ teaspoon ground cinnamon

1½ teaspoons mixed spice

1 teaspoon grated lemon rind

2 tablespoons lemon juice

½ cup (125ml) beef stock

400g (12½ ounces) canned chopped tomatoes

430g (14-ounce) turkish bread (pide)

⅓ cup (50g) pine nuts, toasted (see tips)

¼ cup fresh flat-leaf parsley leaves

¼ cup fresh micro or baby mint leaves

minted yoghurt

200g (6½ ounces) greek-style yoghurt

1 tablespoon chopped fresh mint

1 Preheat oven to 220°C/425°F.

2 Heat 1 tablespoon of the oil in a large frying pan; cook onion and garlic, stirring, for 5 minutes or until onion has softened. Add lamb; cook, stirring, breaking up the lumps with a wooden spoon until lamb is browned. Add spices; stir until fragrant. Add rind, juice, stock and tomatoes; cook, stirring, over medium heat until most of the liquid has evaporated. Remove from heat.

3 Cut bread in half horizontally, place on an oven tray. Drizzle halves with remaining oil; bake for 8 minutes or until lightly golden.

4 Spoon lamb mixture onto bread halves, pressing evenly, leaving a 1cm (¾-inch) border; sprinkle with pine nuts. Cover with foil; bake for 10 minutes. Remove foil; bake for a further 10 minutes or until browned lightly.

5 Meanwhile, make minted yoghurt.

6 Serve pizzas cut into thick slices topped with herbs and minted yoghurt.

minted yoghurt Combine ingredients in a small bowl.

tips Pide (pronounced pih-day) is made from wheat and is usually topped with sesame seeds and fragrant black nigella seeds. Pizza is best baked just before serving; lamb mixture can be made a day ahead or can be frozen for up to 3 months. To toast pine nuts, place in a small dry frying pan over medium heat; stir frequently until browned lightly. Remove from pan immediately. You can serve with tzatziki (see page 51) instead of the minted yoghurt, if you like.

INGREDIENT TIPS

If you like, use coriander (cilantro) instead of thai basil. Any leftover kaffir lime leaves can be frozen for up to 1 month. Fried shallots are available from supermarkets or Asian grocery stores.

PORK LARB WITH LETTUCE & JASMINE RICE

PREP + COOK TIME 25 MINUTES **SERVES** 4

1 tablespoon peanut oil

2 cloves garlic, crushed

600g (1¼ pounds) minced (ground) pork

⅓ cup (90g) grated palm sugar

2 tablespoons fish sauce

4 fresh kaffir lime leaves, sliced finely

½ cup (40g) fried asian shallots

⅓ cup (45g) roasted unsalted peanuts

200g (6½ ounces) packaged microwave jasmine rice

1 butter (boston) lettuce, trimmed, leaves separated

1 tablespoon lime juice

1 cup loosely packed fresh thai basil leaves

1 fresh long red chilli, sliced thinly

2 tablespoons coarsely chopped roasted unsalted peanuts, extra

1 Heat oil in a wok over high heat; stir-fry garlic and pork for 5 minutes or until pork is browned.

2 Add sugar, fish sauce, lime leaves, shallots and peanuts to wok. Reduce heat to low; stir-fry for 2 minutes or until mixture is slightly dry and sticky.

3 Meanwhile, heat rice following packet directions.

4 Remove larb from heat; add juice and three-quarters of the basil.

5 Serve larb with rice and lettuce, topped with chilli, extra chopped peanuts and remaining basil.

tip Palm sugar is usually sold in rock-hard cakes that need to be grated. You can use ¼ cup (55g) firmly packed brown sugar if it's not available.

SLOW-ROASTED LAMB SHOULDER

PREP + COOK TIME 3 HOURS 45 MINUTES **SERVES** 4

Lamb cooked slowly until it's meltingly fall-apart tender – what could be better? Even though it's cooked on the bone, there's no need to worry about carving neat slices; just pull the lamb away in succulent chunks. It's wonderful in winter with roast vegetables but also sensational in summer with a greek salad.

1.3kg (2¾-pound) lamb shoulder, shank on

2 tablespoons olive oil

1kg (2 pounds) potatoes, unpeeled, sliced thickly

2 medium brown onions (300g), unpeeled, sliced thickly

4 drained anchovy fillets, chopped finely

1 garlic bulb (70g)

3 sprigs fresh rosemary

1 cup (250ml) chicken stock

1 cup (250ml) water or dry white wine

1 medium lemon (140g), cut into wedges

1 Preheat oven to 180°C/350°F. Rub lamb all over with salt and freshly ground pepper.

2 Heat oil in a flameproof roasting pan over a medium high heat; cook lamb until browned all over. Remove from pan.

3 Layer potato, onion and anchovies in roasting pan, seasoning with salt and freshly ground pepper between the layers. Cut garlic bulb in half horizontally; place on vegetables.

4 Place lamb on top of vegetables; add rosemary. Pour combined stock and the water over vegetables. Cover pan tightly with two layers of foil. Roast for 1½ hours. Remove foil, reduce oven to 160°C/325°F; roast a further 1½ hours or until the meat can be pulled from the bone easily. Transfer lamb to a tray, cover with foil; rest for 20 minutes. Increase oven to 200°C/400°F.

5 Return vegetables in pan to oven; cook for a further 20 minutes or until browned.

6 Serve lamb with vegetables, garlic and lemon wedges.

tip This is a rustic dish, so there is no need to peel the potatoes or onions. Leaving the skin on keeps these vegetables moist during the long cooking time.

While boneless cuts are easier to slice or carve, the meat tastes better and is more moist when cooked on the bone. A bone-in roast may take a little longer to cook than a boneless roast.

ROAST PORK WITH APPLE SAUCE

PREP + COOK TIME 1 HOUR 25 MINUTES **SERVES** 6

The rind of the pork will crackle better if you leave it unwrapped in the fridge overnight.

6-point rack of pork (1.6kg), rind scored (see tips)

1 tablespoon olive oil

1 tablespoon coarse cooking (kosher) salt

2 teaspoons fennel seeds, crushed

apple sauce

3 large granny smith apples (600g)

½ cup (125ml) water

20g (¾ ounce) butter

1 teaspoon caster (superfine) sugar

½ teaspoon ground cinnamon

1 Preheat oven to 250°C/480°F.

2 Pat the pork dry with paper towel. Place the pork on a rack in a roasting pan. Rub the rind with oil, then with combined salt and crushed fennel seeds.

3 Roast pork for 40 minutes or until the skin blisters. This will probably create smoke in the oven but will give the best crackling result.

4 Reduce oven to 180°C/350°F; roast for a further 35 minutes or until pork is just cooked. To test, insert a meat thermometer into a middle section of the meat; it is cooked when it reaches 62°C/145°F. Or, insert a metal skewer sideways into the thickest part; the juices should run clear.

5 Meanwhile, make apple sauce.

6 Serve pork with apple sauce.

apple sauce Peel and core apples. Cut apples into quarters, then into thick slices. Place apples, the water and butter in a medium saucepan; simmer, uncovered, for 10 minutes or until apple is soft enough to crush with a spoon. Stir in sugar and cinnamon; season.

tips Ask your butcher to score the pork rind for you as it is difficult to do without a sharp Stanley knife or similar. Crush the fennel seeds in a mortar and pestle if you have one, otherwise you can chop them with a knife. Other good pork cuts for roasting: leg roast, boneless rolled loin, loin rack, belly, spare ribs, forequarter roast, shoulder, scotch fillet/neck roast.

serving suggestion Serve with seasonal vegetables such as roast baby (dutch) carrots, potatoes and kumara, brussels sprouts or celeriac and steamed greens.

ROASTING TIMES FOR PORK

With crackling Score the rind at 1cm (½-inch) intervals; rub a little oil and salt well into the scored rind. Roast at 240°C/475°F for 25 minutes. Reduce oven to 180°C/350°F; roast for 20 minutes, per 500g (1 pound).

Without crackling Brown lightly first in a pan all over in a little oil. Roast at 180°C/350°F for 20 minutes, per 500g (1 pound).

Pork belly, shoulder, scotch fillet (neck) Roast, covered, at 180°C/350°F for 3-4 hours, or until the pork is coming away from the bone or is fork-tender.

GLAZED HAM · RECIPE PAGE 62

HONEY GINGER GLAZE

Stir ⅔ cup honey, ½ cup coarsely chopped naked ginger, ½ cup firmly packed brown sugar, ¾ teaspoon ground allspice and ¼ cup water in a small saucepan over a low heat until sugar is dissolved. Process until smooth.

QUINCE GLAZE

Stir 100g (3oz) chopped quince paste and ¼ cup water in a small saucepan over medium heat; bring to boil, stirring for 2 minutes until smooth. Stir in ½ cup honey, 2 teaspoons grated lemon rind and ½ teaspoon ground cumin.

DOUBLE ORANGE GLAZE

Stir 300g (9½oz) orange (or blood orange) marmalade, ¼ cup dark brown sugar and ¼ cup freshly squeezed orange (or blood orange) juice in a small bowl until combined. Season to taste.

APRICOT & MUSTARD GLAZE

Stir 370g (12oz) jar apricot jam, 1 tablespoon white wine vinegar and 2 tablespoons dijon mustard in a small bowl until combined. Season to taste with salt and freshly ground black pepper.

GLAZED HAM

PREP + COOK TIME 2 HOURS **SERVES** 20

Choose from one of the four glazes on page 61 to use with this recipe; we used the double orange glaze. The glazes can be made up to 1 week ahead; store in the fridge. Ham can be glazed a day ahead and served cold. Store leftover ham in the fridge in a ham bag, or wrapped in a cotton or linen tea towel that's been rinsed in water and a little vinegar then wrung out tightly. Change the tea towel daily. The ham will keep for up to 1 week.

8kg (16-pound) cooked leg of ham

2 cups (500ml) water

double orange glaze (see recipe page 61)

sprigs of fresh herbs (rosemary and bay leaves), to decorate

1 Preheat oven to 180°C/350°F. Score through the rind about 10cm (4 inches) from the shank end of the leg.

2 To remove the rind, run your thumb around the edge of the rind just under the skin. Start pulling the rind from the widest edge of the ham; continue to pull the rind carefully away from the fat up to the score line. Remove the rind completely. (Reserved rind can be used to cover the cut surface of the ham to keep it moist during storage.)

3 Using a large sharp knife, score across the fat at 3cm (1¼-inch) intervals, cutting just through the surface of the top fat. Do not cut too deeply or the fat will spread apart during cooking.

4 Place the ham on a wire rack in a large roasting pan; pour 1½ cups of the water into the dish. Brush the ham well with the glaze. Cover the shank end with foil.

5 Bake ham for 1 hour 20 minutes or until browned all over, brushing occasionally with the glaze during cooking, and adding the remaining water if needed.

tips For a smaller leg or half leg of ham, halve the glaze recipes. Rind will remove more easily from the ham if warmed in a low oven (150°C/300°F) for 30 minutes. If the glaze becomes too thick to brush on, reheat until it reaches the correct consistency. The glazes are suitable to microwave in microwave-safe glass or ceramic containers; don't use plastic as the glazes will get very hot.

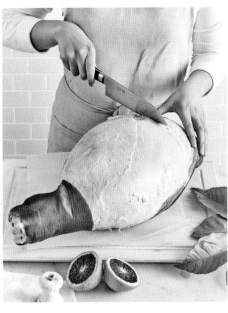

REMOVING THE RIND

Using a small sharp knife, cut through the rind 10cm (4 inches) from the shank end of the leg. Lift rind off in one piece by running your thumb around edge of rind under the skin; pull from the widest edge of the ham up to the shank.

SCORING THE FAT

Using a large sharp knife, score across the fat at about 3cm (1¼-inch) intervals, following the curve of the ham, and cutting just through the surface of the top fat. Do not cut too deeply or the fat will spread apart during cooking.

GLAZING THE HAM

Brush ham well with the glaze. Place ham on a rack in a large roasting pan; add the water. Cover the shank end with foil. Bake for 1 hour 20 minutes or until browned all over, brushing occasionally with the glaze during cooking.

CARVING THE HAM [1]

Place the ham on a chopping board and steady it with a carving fork. Using a large sharp knife, make a vertical cut toward the bone at the shank end then cut a small wedge of ham and remove it. This will provide you with a greater surface area for carving slices.

CARVING THE HAM [2]

Carve towards the bone, taking long sweeps with the knife to get long slices. The pieces of ham will increase in size as you carve. It is best to carve only as much ham as you need at a time, or the meat will dry out.

CARVING THE HAM [3]

Turn the ham over and carve parallel to the bone. The leftover ham bone may be frozen for up to 3 months and used for stock or soup. Keep in mind it will contribute quite a bit of salt to a recipe so additional salt is unlikely to be required.

LAMB MINI ROASTS

PREP + COOK TIME 40 MINUTES **SERVES** 6

⅓ cup (80ml) extra virgin olive oil

2 tablespoons finely chopped fresh rosemary

3 x 350g (11-ounce) lamb rounds, trimmed

800g (1½ pounds) small kumara (orange sweet potato), cut into wedges lengthways

6 sprigs fresh thyme

½ teaspoon dried chilli flakes

200g (6½ ounces) baby green beans

400g (12½ ounces) shelled fresh broad (fava) beans

1 cup (120g) frozen peas

4 chargrilled marinated artichokes, halved

1 tablespoon lemon juice

snow pea sprouts, to serve

anchovy dressing

6 drained anchovies, chopped finely

1 tablespoon baby capers

1 tablespoon red wine vinegar

⅓ cup (80ml) extra virgin olive oil

1 Preheat oven to 200°C/400°F. Combine 1 tablespoon of the oil with rosemary in a large bowl; season with pepper. Add lamb; toss to coat.

2 Heat a medium frying pan over a high heat; cook lamb until browned all over. Transfer to a large roasting pan.

3 Place kumara and another 1 tablespoon of the oil in a small roasting pan; toss to coat. Season. Sprinkle with thyme and chilli.

4 Roast lamb and kumara, on separate shelves: roast lamb for 15 minutes (medium rare) or until done to your liking; and kumara for 25 minutes or until browned and tender. Cover lamb with foil; rest 10 minutes.

5 Meanwhile, make anchovy dressing.

6 Bring a large saucepan of salted water to the boil. Cook green beans for 1 minute, then add broad beans and peas; cook for a further 2 minutes or until just tender. Drain; refresh beans and peas in a bowl of iced water (see tips). Drain. Peel outer skins from the broad beans.

7 Place green and broad beans and peas in a medium bowl with artichokes, juice and remaining oil; toss gently to combine. Season to taste.

8 Place thinly sliced lamb on a warm platter with bean and artichoke salad. Drizzle lamb with anchovy dressing, top with snow pea sprouts; serve with kumara wedges.

anchovy dressing Combine ingredients in a bowl; season to taste.

tips You can buy artichoke hearts from most delis. If fresh broad beans are not available, use frozen ones. For more information on refreshing vegetables, see Vegetable Techniques page 199.

OSSO BUCO

PREP + COOK TIME 2 HOURS 45 MINUTES **SERVES** 8

Veal osso buco, Italian for "bone with a hole", is another name that butchers use for veal shin, usually cut into 3-5cm (1¼-2-inch) thick slices.

2kg (4 pounds) veal osso buco

½ cup (75g) plain (all-purpose) flour

2 tablespoons olive oil

2 medium onions (300g), chopped finely

2 cloves garlic, crushed

½ cup (125ml) dry white wine

700g (1½ pounds) bottled passata (see tip)

1½ cups (375ml) beef stock

gremolata

1 medium lemon (140g)

¼ cup chopped fresh flat-leaf parsley

1 clove garlic, crushed

1 Preheat oven to 170°C/340°F.

2 Coat veal in flour; shake off excess. Heat oil in large flameproof casserole dish over high heat; cook veal, in batches, for 2 minutes each side or until browned. Remove from pan.

3 Cook onion in same dish, stirring over medium-high heat, for 5 minutes or until softened. Add garlic and wine; bring to the boil. Reduce heat; simmer, uncovered, until wine is reduced by half. Add passata and stock; return veal to pan, spoon sauce mixture over veal. Bring to the boil. Cover with a lid or foil. Cook in oven for 2 hours or until the veal is almost falling off the bone.

4 Meanwhile, make gremolata.

5 Serve osso buco sprinkled with gremolata.

gremolata Using a zester, remove rind from lemon into thin strips (or finely grate). Combine rind, parsley and garlic in a small bowl.

tip Passata is sieved pureed tomato, without any added flavourings; sold in bottles or jars in most supermarkets alongside other bottled pasta sauces. If it's not available, puree canned whole tomatoes then push through a sieve to remove any remaining lumps.

serving suggestion Serve with Basic Risotto (page 174) cooked with ½ teaspoon saffron, or with Basic Potato Mash (page 208) and steamed green beans.

BEEF & MUSTARD PIES WITH PEA MASH

PREP + COOK TIME 3 HOURS 30 MINUTES (+ COOLING) **MAKES** 8

2 tablespoons olive oil

1kg (2 pounds) boneless gravy beef, cut into 3cm (1¼-inch) cubes

1 medium onion (150g), chopped finely

2 cloves garlic, crushed

¼ cup (35g) plain (all-purpose) flour

2 tablespoons tomato paste

¼ cup (60ml) dry red wine

3 cups (750ml) beef stock

2 tablespoons dijon mustard

4 sheets puff pastry

2 sheets shortcrust pastry

1 egg, beaten lightly

pea mash

2¼ cups (350g) shelled fresh or frozen peas

2 medium potatoes (400g), chopped coarsely

20g (¾ ounce) butter

1 Heat half the oil in a large saucepan; cook beef, in batches, until well browned. Remove from pan.

2 Heat remaining oil in same pan; cook onion and garlic, stirring, for 5 minutes or until onion is soft. Add flour; cook, stirring, for 1 minute. Stir in paste; cook 1 minute. Gradually stir in wine; cook 1 minute. Gradually stir in stock; cook, stirring, until mixture boils and thickens. Return beef to pan; simmer, covered, for 1¾ hours or

until beef is tender. Strain mixture over a bowl; reserve beef. Return liquid to pan; boil for 15 minutes or until mixture thickens. Return reserved beef to sauce with mustard; stir to combine. Season to taste. Cool.

3 Preheat oven to 200°C/400°F. Grease eight 9cm x 11.5cm (3¾-inch x 4¾-inch) oval pie tins. Using an upturned pie tin as a guide, cut out eight ovals from puff pastry sheets. Refrigerate pastry until needed.

4 Cut shortcrust pastry into quarters to make eight squares. Roll squares out on a floured surface until large enough to line each tin. Ease pastry into tins, press into base and side; trim edges. Prick base with a fork. Line pastry with baking paper; fill with dried beans or rice. Place tins on oven trays. Bake for 10 minutes. Remove beans and paper; bake a further 5 minutes or until browned.

5 Fill pastry cases with beef mixture. Brush edges of pastry with a little egg. Place puff pastry ovals on pies; press edges to seal. Brush tops with a little more egg. Cut a small slit in top of pies to allow steam to escape.

6 Bake pies for 30 minutes or until pastry is golden.

7 Meanwhile, make pea mash.

8 Serve pies with pea mash and, if you like, tomato sauce (ketchup) or chutney.

pea mash Boil, steam or microwave peas and potato, separately, until tender; drain. Process peas until smooth. Mash potato with butter until smooth; season. Stir in peas.

tips Filling and pastry cases can be made a day ahead and baked just before serving. Pies will also keep in an airtight container in the fridge for up to 2 days. They can be frozen uncooked or cooked. Uncooked pies can be baked from frozen. Thaw cooked pies before reheating.

SKEWERS + MARINADES

Use these marinades to flavour 800g (1½ pounds) meat or seafood; we've used pork here. Thread meat onto metal or bamboo skewers; marinate meat for 3 hours (or overnight) in a shallow non-reactive container, and seafood for up to 1 hour. Cook on a preheated chargrill plate or barbecue, turning, for about 5-8 minutes.

CHILLI & KAFFIR LIME

Combine 2 crushed cloves garlic, 4 finely shredded kaffir lime leaves, ⅓ cup fish sauce, 1 small finely chopped fresh red chilli and ⅓ cup peanut oil.

Goes with Pork, chicken, seafood.

THYME & DIJON MUSTARD

Combine ¼ cup lemon juice, ¼ cup extra virgin olive oil, 1 tablespoon dijon mustard, 1 crushed clove garlic and 1 teaspoon thyme leaves.

Goes with Pork, beef, lamb, chicken.

LEMON & OREGANO

Combine ½ cup white wine, ⅓ cup extra virgin olive oil, 2 tablespoons lemon juice, 2 tablespoons fresh oregano leaves and 1 crushed clove garlic.

Goes with Pork, lamb, chicken.

RED WINE

Combine ½ cup red wine, 2 crushed cloves garlic, 1 teaspoon coarsely chopped fresh rosemary and ¼ cup extra virgin olive oil.
Goes with Pork, beef, lamb. For best flavour, marinate overnight.

CHERMOULLA

Combine 2 tablespoons lemon juice, 1 teaspoon each ground cumin, ground coriander and salt, 2 teaspoons sweet paprika, 2 tablespoons olive oil and 2 tablespoons each chopped fresh flat-leaf parsley and coriander (cilantro).
Goes with Pork, beef, lamb, chicken, seafood.

TERIYAKI

Combine ½ cup soy sauce, 2 tablespoons rice wine vinegar, 1 tablespoon brown sugar, 2 crushed cloves garlic and 1 teaspoon finely grated fresh ginger. Sprinkle sesame seeds on cooked skewers.
Goes with Pork, beef, chicken, seafood.

SLOW—COOKER LAMB SHANKS WITH LENTILS

PREP + COOK TIME 8 HOURS 45 MINUTES **SERVES** 4

1½ cups (300g) french-style green lentils

4 french-trimmed lamb shanks (800g)

200g (6½ ounces) bottled caramelised onions

2 medium carrots (240g), cut into 1cm (½-inch) pieces

2 stalks celery (300g), cut into 1cm (½-inch) pieces

2 cloves garlic, crushed

100g (3 ounces) thinly sliced pancetta, chopped coarsely

¼ cup (70g) tomato paste

3 cups (750ml) chicken stock

½ cup (125ml) dry white wine

190g (6 ounces) cavolo nero (tuscan cabbage)

1 Rinse lentils under cold water; drain.
2 Combine lentils, lamb, caramelised onion, carrot, celery, garlic, pancetta, paste, stock and wine in a 5-litre (20-cup) slow cooker. Cook, covered, on low, for 8 hours.
3 Add cavolo nero to cooker; cook, covered, a further 10 minutes. Season to taste.
4 Serve lamb shanks with crusty bread.

tip If you don't have a slow-cooker, follow one of the cooking methods at right.

ON THE STOVE

prep + cook time 4 hours

Heat 1 tablespoon olive oil in a large saucepan over high heat; cook lamb, in batches, until browned. Remove from pan. Heat another 1 tablespoon oil in same pan over low heat; cook pancetta, stirring, until browned. Add carrot and celery; cook, stirring, for 1 minute. Add garlic and paste; cook, stirring, for 1 minute. Add wine; bring to the boil. Boil, uncovered, for 1 minute. Return lamb to pan with caramelised onions and 1 litre (4 cups) stock instead of the 3 cups stock; bring to the boil. Reduce heat; simmer, covered, for 2½ hours. Rinse lentils under cold water; drain. Add lentils to pan; simmer, uncovered, stirring occasionally, for 40 minutes or until lentils and lamb are tender. Add cavolo nero; simmer, for 10 minutes or until cavolo nero is tender. Season to taste.

IN THE OVEN

prep + cook time 4 hours

Preheat oven to 200°C/400°F. Prepare recipe as per ON THE STOVE using the 1 litre (4 cups) chicken stock in a large flameproof casserole dish. Cover dish, transfer to oven; cook for 2½ hours. Add lentils, cover dish; return to oven. Cook for 40 minutes or until lentils and lamb are tender, stirring halfway through cooking time. Add cavolo nero; cook, covered, a further 10 minutes or until cavolo nero is tender. Season to taste.

LAMB & APRICOT TAGINE

PREP + COOK TIME 2 HOURS 20 MINUTES **SERVES** 6

1 tablespoon olive oil

1kg (2 pounds) boned lamb shoulder, trimmed, chopped coarsely

1 medium brown onion (150g), sliced thinly

2 cloves garlic, crushed

1 teaspoon ground cumin

1 teaspoon ground coriander

1 teaspoon ground cinnamon

2 cups (500ml) beef stock

½ cup (75g) coarsely chopped dried apricots

100g (3 ounces) baby spinach leaves

¼ cup (40g) blanched whole almonds, roasted

1 Heat half the oil in a large saucepan; cook lamb, in batches, until well browned. Remove from pan.
2 Heat remaining oil in same pan; cook onion and garlic, stirring, until onion softens. Add spices; cook, stirring, until fragrant. Return lamb to pan with stock; bring to the boil. Reduce heat; simmer, covered, for 1 hour 40 minutes.
3 Add apricots; simmer, covered, a further 20 minutes or until lamb is tender. Stir in spinach; season to taste.
4 Serve tagine sprinkled with nuts.

tips If you have a pressure cooker, this recipe can become a weekday dinner. Always check with the manufacturer's instructions before using a pressure cooker. Use ¾ cup (180ml) stock instead of 2 cups then bring a 6-litre (24-cup) pressure cooker to high pressure. Reduce heat to stabilise pressure; cook for 25 minutes. Release pressure using the quick release method; remove lid. Add apricots; secure lid. Bring cooker to high pressure. Reduce heat to stabilise pressure; cook about 2 minutes. Release pressure using the quick release method; remove lid. Stir in spinach; season to taste. Tagine is suitable to freeze.
serving suggestion Serve with Basic Couscous (see page 192).

SLOW-COOKER MASSAMAN BEEF CURRY

PREP + COOK TIME 8 HOURS 45 MINUTES **SERVES** 6

2 tablespoons peanut oil

2 large onions (400g), cut into thin wedges

1kg (2 pounds) gravy beef, cut into 5cm (2-inch) pieces

⅔ cup (200g) massaman curry paste

1 cup (250ml) coconut milk

1 cup (250ml) beef stock

2 cinnamon sticks

2 dried bay leaves

3 medium potatoes (600g), chopped coarsely

2 tablespoons brown sugar

1 tablespoons fish sauce

½ cup (70g) roasted unsalted peanuts

1 long green onion (scallion), sliced thinly

⅓ cup lightly packed fresh coriander leaves (cilantro)

1 lime, cut into wedges

1 Heat half the oil in large frying pan; cook onion, stirring, for 10 minutes or until browned lightly. Transfer to a 4.5-litre (18-cup) slow cooker.

2 Heat remaining oil in same pan; cook beef, in batches, until browned. Add paste; cook, stirring, 1 minute or until fragrant. Transfer to cooker.

3 Add coconut milk, stock, cinnamon, bay leaves and potato to cooker. Cook, covered, on low, for 8 hours.

4 Stir in sugar and sauce. Serve curry topped with peanuts, green onion and coriander; serve with lime wedges.

tip Chuck steak is also suitable for this recipe. If you don't have a slow-cooker, follow the cooking method below.

ON THE STOVE

prep + cook time 2 hours 30 minutes

Heat half the oil in a large saucepan; cook onion, stirring, 10 minutes or until browned lightly. Transfer to a bowl. Heat remaining oil in same pan; cook beef, in batches, until well browned. Add paste; cook, stirring, for 1 minute or until fragrant. Return onion to pan with coconut milk, 2 cups stock instead of 1 cup, cinnamon and bay leaves. Bring to the boil; simmer, covered, for 1½ hours. Add potato; simmer, covered, for a further 30 minutes or until beef and potato are tender, adding a little extra stock or water if necessary. Stir in sugar and sauce.

CHICKEN

CHICKEN WINGS

To make chicken wing nibbles for fingerfood,
snip the tips off wings using strong kitchen
scissors, then cut the wings in half at the joint
with the scissors or a large flat knife. Trimmings
can be saved and frozen to make stocks in
the future (see Basic Stocks page 226).
Cook the chicken wing nibbles scattered with
a spice rub (see pages 94 & 95) or with
a sticky marinade (see pages 102 & 103).

QUICKER COOKING

Chicken marylands are chicken thighs with
the drumstick attached; they are suited to
barbecuing and roasting rather than pan-frying,
or a combination of pan-frying to brown and then
finished off in the oven. To speed up the cooking
time make three deep cuts, to the bone, into the
thickest part of drumsticks and thighs. If the
chicken is marinated or covered in a spice rub,
the flavour will penetrate into the cuts.

BUTTERFLYING A CHICKEN

Butterflying is technique used to flatten poultry so that it can cook evenly and more quickly with direct heat cooking methods such as barbecuing. To butterfly a whole chicken or spatchcock (young chicken), place breast-side-down on a board. Cut down either side of the backbone with strong kitchen scissors. Discard backbone or freeze to make stock in (see Basic Stocks page 226). Turn over, press firmly with the heel of your hand to flatten.

POUNDING CHICKEN BREASTS

To make chicken escalopes (thin slices of chicken) to crumb for chicken schnitzels, start by removing the chicken tenderloin from the underside of the chicken breast, don't discard it as it can also be crumbed. Holding a sharp knife horizontally, split the chicken breast in half horizontally. Place the two pieces between baking paper or plastic wrap; pound using the flat side of a meat mallet, or use the side of a rolling pin until even in thickness.

CHICKEN

CRUMBED CHICKEN WITH SPICY MAYONNAISE

PREP + COOK TIME 25 MINUTES **SERVES** 4

½ cup (75g) plain (all-purpose) flour

2 eggs

1 cup (75g) panko (japanese) breadcrumbs

½ cup (40g) finely grated parmesan

¼ cup coarsely chopped fresh flat-leaf parsley

2 teaspoons finely grated lemon rind

12 chicken tenderloins (900g)

vegetable oil, for shallow-frying

3 cups (75g) mixed salad leaves

2 teaspoons lemon juice

lemon wedges, to serve

spicy mayonnaise

⅔ cup (200g) whole-egg mayonnaise

¾ teaspoon piri piri seasoning

2 teaspoons lemon juice

1 Make spicy mayonnaise.

2 Place flour in shallow bowl; season with salt and freshly ground black pepper. Lightly beat eggs in another shallow bowl. Combine breadcrumbs, parmesan, parsley and rind in a third shallow bowl. Dust chicken in flour; dip in egg, allowing excess to drip off, then coat in breadcrumb mixture.

3 Heat 1cm (½-inch) oil in a large frying pan over medium heat; shallow-fry chicken, in batches, for 1 minute each side or until golden and cooked through. Remove with a slotted spoon; drain on paper towel.

4 Place salad leaves in a medium bowl with lemon juice; toss gently to combine.

5 Serve chicken with spicy mayonnaise, salad leaves and lemon wedges.

spicy mayonnaise Combine ingredients in a small bowl.

tip The spicy mayonnaise and chicken can be prepared up to the end of step 2, 4 hours ahead; refrigerate, separately, covered.

PORTUGUESE PIRI PIRI CHICKEN

PREP + COOK TIME 45 MINUTES **SERVES** 4

This is a moderately spicy recipe, which can be tamed for milder tastes by removing all the seeds from the chillies, the part the contributes the most heat.

2 medium desiree potatoes (400g)

1.6kg (3¼-pound) butterflied chicken (see tips)

⅓ cup (80ml) vegetable oil

½ cup (150g) mayonnaise

piri piri sauce

6 fresh long red chillies

1 teaspoon finely grated lemon rind

2 tablespoons lemon juice

4 cloves garlic, halved

2 teaspoons sweet paprika

¼ cup coarsely chopped fresh oregano

½ cup (125ml) olive oil

1 Preheat oven to 200°C/400°F.

2 Make piri piri sauce.

3 Prick potatoes all over with a fork. Microwave on HIGH (100%) for 3 minutes or until potatoes are tender. Cut into 4cm (1½-inch) pieces.

4 Rub ⅓ cup piri piri sauce on both sides of chicken. Heat oil in a large flameproof roasting pan over medium-high heat; cook chicken, skin-side down, for 5 minutes. Turn chicken over. Add potato to pan; cook a for further 5 minutes, turning potato until golden. Transfer pan to oven; roast for 25 minutes or until chicken juices run clear when the thickest part of a thigh is pierced.

5 Combine mayonnaise with remaining piri piri sauce.

6 Serve chicken and potato on a platter with piri piri mayonnaise. If you like, top with fresh oregano leaves.

piri piri sauce Halve 3 chillies lengthways; remove then discard seeds. Coarsely chop all chillies; process with remaining ingredients until well combined. Season well with salt.

tips Ask the butcher to butterfly the chicken for you, or see Chicken Techniques page 81 to try it yourself. You can use other cuts of chicken on the bone, such as wings, thigh cutlets and marylands.

serving suggestion Serve with green salad leaves and grilled lemon halves. Brush oil on cut sides of lemon; place, cut-side down, in a heated grill pan or on barbecue for 2 minutes until lightly charred.

RECIPE VARIATION

For a vegetarian option, swap the chicken for firm tofu. Pat tofu dry with paper towel, cut into 1cm (½-inch) thick slices. Marinate as in step 1 of the recipe; cook for 2 minutes each side or until golden.

LEMON GRASS & CHICKEN BANH MI BOWL

PREP + COOK TIME 30 MINUTES (+ REFRIGERATION) **SERVES** 4

800g (1½ pounds) small chicken thigh fillets

¼ cup lemon grass paste (see tips)

1 teaspoon dried chilli flakes

1½ tablespoons vegetable oil

2 medium carrots (240g), cut into matchsticks (see tips)

300g (9½ ounces) daikon, cut into matchsticks (see tips)

½ cup (125ml) white wine vinegar

1 tablespoon caster (superfine) sugar

500g (1 pound) packaged microwave white rice

2 tablespoons light soy sauce

4 green onions (scallions), sliced thinly

2 lebanese cucumbers (260g), cut into wedges

⅔ cup loosely packed fresh coriander (cilantro) leaves

½ cup (150g) mayonnaise

¼ cup (70g) sriracha chilli sauce (see tips)

2 limes (180g), cut into cheeks

1 Combine chicken, lemon grass paste, chilli and oil in a large bowl; season. Cover; refrigerate for 30 minutes.
2 Meanwhile, combine carrot, daikon, vinegar and sugar in a medium bowl, season; stand for 5 minutes. Drain.
3 Cook chicken on a heated oiled grill plate (or barbecue) for 3 minutes each side or until cooked through. Cut chicken thickly widthways.
4 Heat rice following packet instructions. Divide rice into serving bowls, drizzle with soy sauce. Top with chicken, pickled vegetables, green onion, cucumber and coriander.
5 Combine mayonnaise and sriracha in a small bowl.
6 Serve banh mi bowls with sriracha mayonnaise and lime cheeks.

tips Lemon grass paste is available from the fresh food section of major supermarkets. To cut carrots and daikon into matchsticks, see General Techniques page 228. Sriracha is a thai-style chilli sauce available from selected supermarkets and Asian food stores. Substitute with whatever chilli sauce you have on hand, or use a little fresh seeded chilli.

DRUMSTICKS WITH SPICE RUBS

Preheat oven to 200°F/400°F. Rub ¼ cup the chosen spice rub mix all over 12 chicken drumsticks (1.8kg).
Place chicken on a baking-paper-lined oven tray; season with salt. Roast for 45 minutes or until chicken is
cooked through. The dry spice rub will keep for 3 months in an airtight jar in a cool, dark place.

INDIAN-STYLE RUB

Place 2 tablespoons each of coriander seeds and cumin seeds in a
small frying pan over medium heat; cook, stirring, for 40 seconds
or until fragrant. Transfer to a mortar and pestle, cool; grind finely.
Stir in 2 teaspoons each ground turmeric and medium-hot curry
powder and 1 teaspoon each ground ginger and ground chilli.
Serve cooked drumsticks with fresh coriander (cilantro) leaves.

SMOKY SPICE RUB

Place 1 tablespoon each of fennel seeds, cumin seeds and
coriander seeds in a small frying pan over medium heat; cook,
stirring constantly, for 45 seconds or until fragrant. Transfer
to a mortar and pestle, cool; grind finely. Stir in 1 tablespoon
each smoked paprika and finely grated lemon rind.
Serve cooked drumsticks with fresh thyme and lemon cheeks.

SUMAC RUB

Place 1 tablespoon whole black peppercorns and 1 teaspoon each onion flakes and sea salt flakes in a mortar and pestle; grind until finely ground. Transfer to a medium bowl; stir in 2 tablespoons sumac, 1 tablespoon dried oregano and 1 teaspoon garlic powder. Serve cooked drumsticks wtih fresh oregano leaves.

CAJUN RUB

Combine 1½ tablespoons mild paprika, 3 teaspoons dried basil leaves, 1 teaspoon each ground black pepper and ground fennel seeds, ½ teaspoon each dried thyme and ground white pepper and a pinch chilli powder (or to taste). Serve cooked drumsticks with fresh basil leaves and lime wedges.

Chicken Satay Skewers

PREP + COOK TIME 20 MINUTES (+ REFRIGERATION) **SERVES** 4

8 chicken thigh fillets (1.2kg), cut into 2cm (¾-inch) pieces

1 teaspoon curry powder

½ teaspoon onion powder

½ teaspoon garlic powder

¼ teaspoon ground cumin

¼ teaspoon ground chilli

2 tablespoons peanut oil

1 large onion (200g), grated

2 teaspoons grated fresh ginger

1 cup (250ml) coconut cream

¾ cup (210g) crunchy peanut butter

2 tablespoons sweet chilli sauce

2 tablespoons light soy sauce

¼ cup (35g) crushed roasted peanuts

450g (14½ ounces) packaged microwave white rice

1 telegraph cucumber (400g), cut into wedges

1 fresh small red chilli, seeded, sliced thinly

1 Combine chicken, spices and half the oil in a large bowl; season. Cover; refrigerate for 1 hour.

2 Heat an oiled chargrill plate (or grill pan or barbecue).

3 Thread chicken onto 12 skewers (see Tips About Skewers opposite). Cook skewers for 3 minutes each side or until chicken is cooked through.

4 Meanwhile, heat remaining oil in a small saucepan; cook onion and ginger, stirring, for 1 minute or until onion softens. Add coconut cream, peanut butter, sauces and peanuts; simmer, stirring, for 1 minute. (Sauce may separate on standing, but will come back together again when stirred before serving.)

5 Heat rice according to packet directions.

6 Serve chicken skewers with peanut sauce, rice, cucumber wedges and chilli. If you like, serve with lime cheeks and top with fresh coriander (cilantro) leaves.

TIPS ABOUT SKEWERS

Metal skewers accelerate cooking as they heat the surrounding food. Bamboo skewers should be soaked in water for 20 minutes to prevent them scorching during cooking.

COOKING NOTES

Cooking chicken in both butter and oil allows you to cook at a higher temperature than if you were to use butter alone, which might burn. You could simply use oil, however the butter adds a lovely golden colour and flavour to the pan juices.

CHICKEN & ROSEMARY SALTIMBOCCA

PREP + COOK TIME 25 MINUTES **SERVES** 4

250g (8 ounces) truss cherry tomatoes

2 tablespoons olive oil

4 x 180g (5½-ounce) chicken breast fillets

4 slices prosciutto (60g)

4 long sprigs rosemary

4 wooden toothpicks

30g (1 ounce) butter

¼ cup (60ml) dry white wine

1 Preheat grill (broiler) to high.

2 Place tomatoes on an oven tray; drizzle with half the oil. Cook under the grill for 5 minutes or until skins split.

3 Meanwhile, place chicken breasts, one at a time, between sheets of plastic wrap; pound with the flat side of a meat mallet until even in thickness. Alternatively, pound with a wooden rolling pin.

4 Place a piece of prosciutto and a rosemary sprig on top of each chicken breast and secure with a toothpick.

5 Heat remaining oil and the butter in a large frying pan over medium-high heat; cook chicken, rosemary-side down, for 3 minutes or until lightly browned. Turn over; cook for a further 3 minutes or until cooked through. Transfer to a plate; cover and keep warm.

6 Add wine to same pan; bring to the boil. Boil for 1 minute or until thickened slightly. Season.

7 Remove toothpicks from chicken. Serve chicken with grilled tomatoes and drizzled with pan juices.

serving suggestion Serve with a green leaf salad.

CHILLI CHICKEN SAN CHOY BOW

PREP + COOK TIME 20 MINUTES **SERVES** 6

1 tablespoon peanut oil

2 cloves garlic, crushed

2 teaspoons finely grated fresh ginger

4 fresh long red chillies, chopped finely

1kg (2 pounds) minced (ground) chicken

½ cup (125ml) oyster sauce

230g (7 ounces) canned sliced water chestnuts, drained, rinsed, chopped finely

2 cups (160g) bean sprouts

4 green onions (scallions), sliced thinly

12 iceberg lettuce leaves (see tips)

⅓ cup (50g) roasted unsalted cashews

sliced chilli and baby coriander (cilantro), to serve

1 Heat oil in a large, deep frying pan; cook garlic, ginger and chilli, stirring, over high heat, for 1 minute or until fragrant.

2 Add chicken to the pan; cook, stirring, until browned. Add sauce, chestnuts, sprouts and onion; stir until heated through.

3 Spoon chicken mixture into lettuce leaves; sprinkle with nuts. Accompany with lemon wedges and sliced chilli and baby coriander, if you like.

tips You will need about 2 iceberg lettuces for this recipe; see cooking notes opposite for more tips. For speed, you can process garlic, ginger and chilli in a small food processor until finely chopped.

CHICKEN & SNAKE BEAN STIR-FRY

PREP + COOK TIME 20 MINUTES **SERVES** 4

⅔ cup (130g) jasmine rice

1 tablespoon peanut oil

800g (1½ pounds) chicken thigh fillets, sliced thickly

2 medium onions (300g), sliced thickly

3 cloves garlic, crushed

1 teaspoon chinese five spice powder

400g (12½ ounces) snake beans, cut into 5cm (2-inch) lengths

½ cup (125ml) oyster sauce

2 tablespoons light soy sauce

½ cup (75g) cashews, roasted

½ cup loosely packed fresh thai basil leaves

1 fresh long red chilli, sliced thinly on the diagonal

1 Cook rice in a saucepan of boiling water for 12 minutes or until tender; drain.

2 Heat half the oil in a wok over high heat; stir-fry chicken, in batches, until browned all over and cooked through. Remove from wok.

3 Heat remaining oil in wok; stir-fry onion, garlic and five spice for 3 minutes or until onion softens. Add beans; stir-fry for 4 minutes or until tender.

4 Return chicken to wok with sauces and cashews; stir-fry until sauce boils and thickens slightly.

5 Just before serving, stir in basil. Serve stir-fry with rice; top with chilli.

serving suggestion Serve with rice noodles instead of rice, if you like.

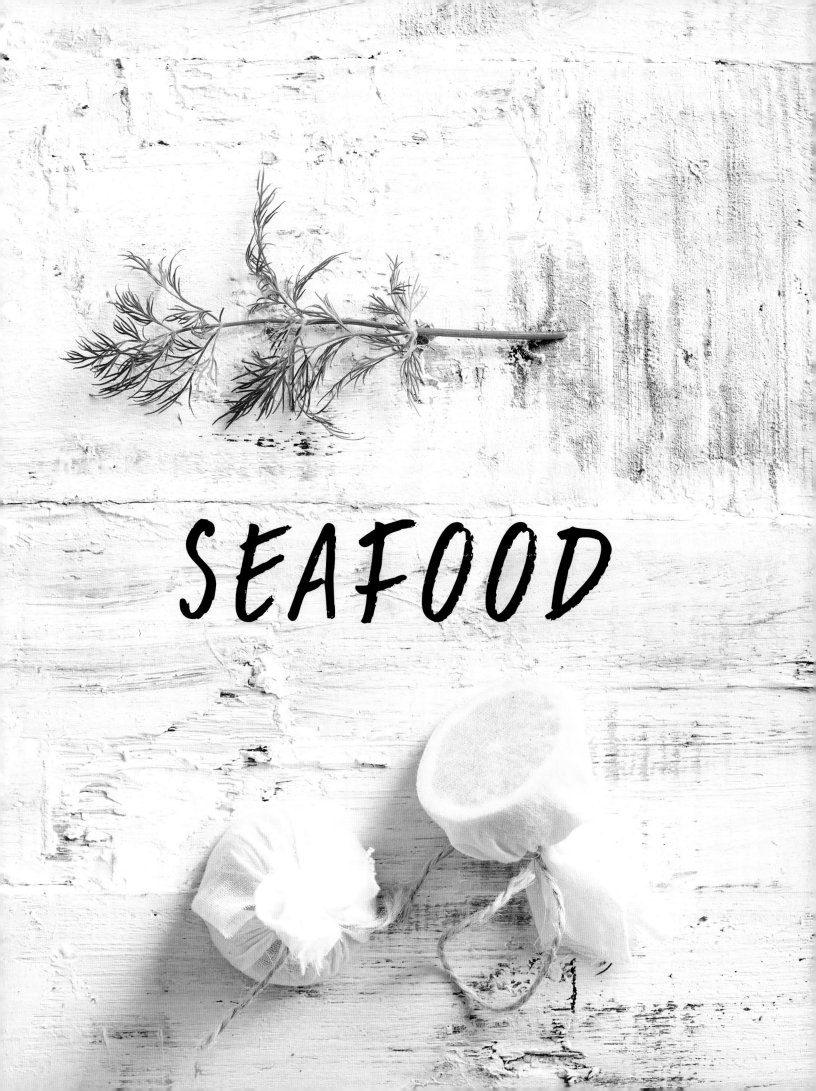

SEAFOOD

SHELLING & DEVEINING PRAWNS

Twist or cut behind the prawn head to remove it. Peel away the shell starting from legs. You can leave the last segment of shell on to leave the tail intact for presentation. To devein, make a small cut in the centre back of prawns. Insert a skewer or toothpick through the skin and under the vein, then lift; this will pull the vein out in one piece. Alternatively, run a small knife down the back of the prawn to expose the vein and pull it out that way.

SLASHING FISH

Cutting deep slashes into the thickest part of a fish helps to cook fish evenly and more quickly. It also helps to absorb flavours into the flesh. Using a sharp knife, make three parallel cuts approximately 3cm (1¼ inches) apart. As the slashes make the flesh visible you will be able to tell very easily when the fish is cooked. To check when the fish is cooked, use a small knife to prise the flesh apart down to the bone – the flesh will change from opaque to white when cooked.

CLEANING SQUID

To clean whole squid (also known as calamari), pull the head and entrails from squid body. Remove and discard the clear "quill" inside, running the length of the body or hood. Cut the tentacles from the head, just below the eyes then remove the hard black beak in the centre. Pull away the membrane from the hood and flaps; wash the hood, tentacles and flaps well. To assist with gripping the squid you can dip your fingers into a little salt. Cut the squid hoods into narrower lengths. So that they curl during cooking, score the inside in a criss-cross pattern with a sharp knife.

CLEANING MUSSELS

Two steps are necssary before you can cook mussels: scrubbing and bearding. Firstly, discard any mussels that open and those with cracked shells. Scrub the shells with a strong scourer to remove any debris that is attached. Wash the mussels under plenty of cold water. Visible between the mussel shells you will see attached the rope-like tough fibrous beard. To remove it, pull down firmly and jerk it away from the shell.

CRISP SKIN
SALMON FILLETS

Rub 4 salmon fillets, skin on, with 1 tablespoon olive oil. Season
all over with salt. Cook salmon, skin-side down, in a heated
frying pan or on a barbecue flatplate for 4 minutes or until skin
is crisp and browned. Turn, cook for a further minute or until
done as desired. Salmon is best served a little rare in the centre.
Serve with lemon halves or one of the toppings opposite.

NAM JIM

Process 3 peeled cloves garlic, 3 fresh long green chillies, seeded, chopped coarsely, ¼ cup fresh coriander (cilantro) leaves, 2 coriander roots, 2 tablespoons fish sauce, 2 tablespoons grated palm sugar, 3 chopped shallots and ¼ cup lime juice until smooth; season to tatse. Serve on crisp skin salmon fillets with extra coriander leaves and lime wedges.

SALSA VERDE

Process 2 cups firmly packed fresh flat-leaf parsley leaves, 1½ tablespoons loosely packed fresh lemon thyme leaves, 1 tablespoon capers, 1 crushed clove garlic, 1 teaspoon caster (superfine) sugar, ½ cup olive oil and 1½ tablespoons white wine vinegar until combined. Season to taste. Serve on crisp skin salmon fillets with extra thyme and char-grilled lemon halves.

GREEN MANGO RELISH

Stir 1½ tablespoons each grated palm sugar and fish sauce in a small saucepan over low heat until sugar has dissolved. Cool 5 minutes. Combine 1 coarsely grated green mango with 1½ tablespoons lime juice, 2 chopped shallots and 1 thinly sliced small red chilli. Add sugar mixture; toss gently. Serve on crisp skin salmon fillets with extra chilli, if you like.

CHERMOULLA YOGHURT

Process ½ cup each firmly packed fresh flat-leaf parsley and coriander (cilantro) leaves, 2 chopped cloves garlic, 1 teaspoon each chilli flakes, ground cumin and ground coriander until combined. Add 1 tablespoon each lemon juice and olive oil; process until smooth. Stir in ½ cup greek-style yoghurt; season. Serve on crisp skin salmon fillets with extra flat-leaf parsley.

SEAFOOD LAKSA

PREP + COOK TIME 35 MINUTES **SERVES** 4

500g (1 pound) uncooked medium king prawns (shrimp)

375g (12 ounces) dried rice vermicelli noodles

185g (6 ounces) bottled laksa paste (see tip)

3¼ cups (800ml) coconut milk

1½ cups (375ml) water

2 tablespoons peanut oil

750g (1½ pounds) fresh marinara mix

12 fried tofu puffs (105g), halved

1½ cups (120g) bean sprouts

¼ cup (20g) fried shallots

1 long fresh red chilli, sliced thinly

⅓ cup loosely packed fresh coriander (cilantro) leaves

1 lime (90g), cut into wedges

1 Shell and devein prawns, leaving the tails intact (see Seafood Techniques page 110).

2 Place noodles in a medium heatproof bowl, cover with boiling water. Stand for 1½ minutes or until almost tender; drain.

3 Meanwhile, cook paste in a large saucepan over medium heat, stirring, for 3 minutes or until fragrant. Stir in coconut milk and the water; bring to a simmer over medium heat.

4 Heat oil in a large frying pan over high heat; cook marinara mix and prawns, in batches, for 2 minutes or until just changed in colour.

5 Add seafood and tofu to laksa mixture; simmer, stirring occasionally, for 2 minutes or seafood is just cooked.

6 Divide noodles among bowls; top with laksa mixture. Sprinkle with sprouts, shallots, chilli and coriander. Serve with lime wedges.

tip Supermarket laksa pastes are generally mild so you may like to add extra chilli or a couple tablespoons chilli sauce such as sriracha, if you prefer a hotter spice level. Laksa pastes from Asian grocers that look drier and thick are generally much hotter, in which case use ½ cup paste. Use an amount that suits your heat tolerance level.

WHOLE FISH WITH GINGER & GREEN ONIONS

PREP + COOK TIME 35 MINUTES **SERVES** 4

Other fish to try whole are: barramundi, bream and river trout. Allow about 400g (12½ ounces) per person, and adjust the number of fish depending on their size.

2 x 800g (1½-pound) whole snapper, cleaned

¼ teaspoon ground white pepper

8cm (3¼-inch) piece fresh ginger, peeled, cut into long thin strips

3 green onions (scallions), trimmed, sliced thinly

2 tablespoons light soy sauce

2 tablespoons chinese cooking wine (shao hsing)

½ teaspoon caster (superfine) sugar

1 teaspoon sesame oil

1 long fresh red chilli, seeded, sliced thinly on the diagonal

2 tablespoons peanut oil

1 cup loosely packed fresh coriander (cilantro) leaves

1 Preheat oven to 200°C/400°F.

2 Pat fish dry with paper towel then make three deep cuts through the flesh on each side (see Seafood Techniques page 110).

3 Take four large sheets of baking paper and rinse under cold water to make the paper pliable. Place two sheets in a cross pattern on each of two oven trays; place a fish in the centre of each. Sprinkle both sides of the fish with pepper; top with half the ginger and the white part of the green onion. Bring the sides of the paper together and seal by folding over, then wrap over the remaining sides, tucking the short sides under to form a sealed parcel.

4 Bake fish for 20 minutes. To test if the fish is cooked, check in one of the cuts; the flesh should be white. Insert a fork into the thickest part; the flesh should come away from the bone easily.

5 Meanwhile, stir soy sauce, cooking wine, sugar and sesame oil in a small bowl until sugar dissolves.

6 Transfer fish to a platter; top with chilli, drizzle with soy dressing.

7 Heat peanut oil in a small saucepan, add remaining ginger; cook, stirring for 2 minutes or until golden. Spoon oil and ginger over fish. Top with coriander.

tips You can use 4 plate-sized fish and wrap each individually, if you prefer, so each diner gets their own parcel. Check if the fish is ready after 12 minutes cooking time.

serving suggestion Serve with steamed rice and greens, such as buk choy, choy sum, broccolini or snow peas.

PERFECT FISH 'N' CHIPS

PREP + COOK TIME 50 MINUTES (+ REFRIGERATION & STANDING) **SERVES** 4

vegetable oil, for deep-frying

750g (1½ pounds) potatoes, peeled

750g (1½ pounds) firm white fish fillets, cut into 8 pieces

⅓ cup (50g) cornflour (cornstarch)

batter

1½ cups (225g) self-raising flour

½ cup (75g) cornflour (cornstarch)

1½ cups (375ml) chilled beer

¼ cup (60ml) chilled soda water

tartare sauce

½ cup (150g) whole-egg mayonnaise

1 tablespoon lemon juice

2 teaspoons capers, chopped

1 tablespoon finely chopped dill pickles

1 tablespoon finely chopped fresh dill

1 Make batter, then tartare sauce.

2 Cut potatoes lengthways into 1.5cm (¾-inch) thick slices; cut each slice lengthways into 1.5cm (¾-inch) thick chips. Place chips in a bowl of iced water while preparing remaining potatoes to prevent discolouration.

3 Pat chips dry with paper towel. Heat oil in a large saucepan over medium-high heat; cook chips, in two batches, for 4 minutes or until just tender but not browned. Drain on paper towel; stand 10 minutes.

4 Reheat oil; recook chips, in batches, until crisp and golden brown. Drain on paper towel.

5 Toss fish in flour; shake away any excess. Dip fish in batter; drain off excess.

6 Reheat oil; cook fish, in batches, for 4 minutes or until golden and just cooked through. Drain on paper towel.

batter Sift flours into a large bowl; gradually whisk in beer and soda water to form a thin batter.

tartare sauce Combine ingredients in a small bowl.

tips Rinse cut potatoes in cold water to remove starch. Drain well; pat dry with a clean tea towel. You can use any firm white fish you prefer, such as whiting, flathead, snapper or bream.

serving suggestion Serve with lemon wedges or halves.

OIL TEMPERATURE

Cooking thermometer
Heat oil to 165°C/325°F for the first frying of the chips. Increase to 180°C/350°F for the second frying of the chips and for frying the fish. (See also General Techniques page 229.)

PRAWN CHU CHEE CURRY

PREP + COOK TIME 1 HOUR **SERVES** 6

¼ cup (60g) ghee (see tip)

2½ tablespoons thai red curry paste

1kg (2 pounds) uncooked prawns (shrimp),
shelled and deveined with tails intact
(see Seafood Techniques page 110)

6 fresh kaffir lime leaves

270ml coconut milk

1 cup (250ml) chicken stock

2 tablespoons brown or palm sugar

2 tablespoons fish sauce

1 tablespoon tamarind puree

1 cup (170g) chopped fresh pineapple

250g (8 ounces) grape tomatoes

1 fresh long red chilli, seeded, shredded finely

coconut rice

1 cup (75g) shredded coconut

1 tablespoon shredded fresh ginger

30g (1 ounce) ghee (see tip)

500g (1 pound) packaged microwave brown rice

1 Make coconut rice.

2 Heat ghee in a wok over medium-high heat. Add paste;
cook, stirring, for 2 minutes. Add prawns and 3 crushed
lime leaves; cook, stirring, for 2 minutes. Add sugar,
sauce and tamarind. Stir in tomato and pineapple;
cook for a further 2 minutes or until warmed through.

3 Finely shred remaining lime leaves; combine with
chilli. Sprinkle lime leaf mixture on curry; serve with
coconut rice.

coconut rice Place coconut in a medium frying pan
over medium heat; stir continuously for 3 minutes or
until golden. Remove from pan. Heat half the ghee in
same pan, add ginger; cook, stirring, for 3 minutes or
until golden. Add toasted coconut and rice; cook,
stirring, for 3 minutes or until heated through.

tip Ghee is clarified butter, meaning the milk solids
have been removed. The lack of milk solids gives this
fat a high smoking point so it can be heated to a high
temperature without burning. It is available from most
large supermarkets.

STEAMED MUSSELS

PREP + COOK TIME 25 MINUTES **SERVES** 4

2kg (4 pounds) black mussels • 40g (1½ ounces) butter •
6 cloves garlic, chopped • 8 green onions (scallions),
sliced finely • 1 cup (250ml) white wine • ½ cup chopped
fresh flat-leaf parsley

Scrub mussels under cold water; remove beards (see
Seafood Techniques page 111). Melt butter in a large
saucepan over a medium heat; cook garlic and green
onion, stirring, for 1 minute or until soft. Increase heat to
medium-high; add mussels and wine. Cover; bring to the
boil. Reduce heat; cook, covered, for 5 minutes, shaking
pan occasionally. Remove pan from heat. Toss through
parsley. Serve with crusty bread to mop up the broth.

TOMATO CHILLI MUSSELS

Heat 40g (1½oz) butter in a large saucepan over medium heat; cook 2 crushed cloves garlic, 1 finely chopped medium onion and 2 sliced fresh long red chillies until onion is soft. Add 800g (1½lb) canned chopped tomatoes; bring to the boil. Add 2kg (4lb) cleaned black mussels to pan. Cover; cook for 5 minutes until mussels open.

THAI-STYLE MUSSELS

Stir 2 tablespoons thai green curry paste in a large saucepan over medium heat until fragrant. Add 1½ cups each fish stock and water, 1 tablespoon fish sauce and 2 teaspoons brown sugar; bring to the boil. Add 2kg (4lb) cleaned black mussels. Cover, cook for 5 minutes until mussels open. Add 400ml coconut milk, stir until hot. Serve with sliced green chilli and lime wedges.

CHORIZO MUSSELS

Cook 200g (6½oz) sliced chorizo in large pan until browned. Remove. Cook 2 teaspoons sweet paprika in pan until fragrant; stir in 400g (12½oz) canned chopped tomatoes, pinch of sugar and 1 cup chicken stock; bring to the boil. Add 2kg (4lb) cleaned black mussels. Cover, cook 5 minutes or until mussels open. Stir in chorizo and chopped flat-leaf parsley. Serve with lemon wedges.

BEER & THYME MUSSELS

Heat 1 tablespoon olive oil in a large saucepan; cook 1 finely chopped onion, 4 crushed cloves garlic and 3 sprigs thyme until soft. Add 1½ cups beer; bring to the boil. Add 2kg (4lb) cleaned black mussels. Cover, cook for 5 minutes or until mussels open. Remove mussels. Add 60g (2oz) chopped butter to pan, stir until combined. Season. Pour over mussels.

PAD THAI

PREP + COOK TIME 40 MINUTES (+ STANDING) **SERVES** 4

¼ cup (85g) tamarind puree

2 tablespoons grated palm sugar

⅓ cup (80ml) sweet chilli sauce

⅓ cup (80ml) fish sauce

375g (12 ounces) rice stick noodles

12 uncooked medium prawns (shrimp) (500g)

2 cloves garlic, crushed

2 fresh small red chillies, chopped coarsely

2 tablespoons dried shrimp

1 tablespoon grated fresh ginger

1 tablespoon peanut oil

250g (8 ounces) minced (ground) pork

3 eggs, beaten lightly

2 cups (160g) bean sprouts

4 green onions (scallions), sliced thinly, white and green parts separated

¼ cup (35g) coarsely chopped roasted unsalted peanuts

⅓ cup coarsely chopped fresh coriander (cilantro)

1 medium lemon (140), cut into wedges

1 Combine tamarind, sugar and sauces in a small bowl.

2 Place noodles in a large heatproof bowl; cover with boiling water. Stand until just tender; drain.

3 Shell and devein prawns, leaving tails intact (see Seafood Techniques, page 110).

4 Blend or process garlic, chilli, shrimp and ginger until mixture forms a paste.

5 Heat oil in a wok; stir-fry garlic paste until fragrant. Add pork; stir-fry until just cooked through. Add prawns; stir-fry for 1 minute. Add egg; stir-fry until egg just sets. Add noodles, tamarind mixture, sprouts and white part of the green onion; stir-fry, tossing gently to combine.

6 Remove wok from heat, add remaining green onion with peanuts and coriander; toss gently until combined. Serve with lemon wedges.

SALT AND PEPPER SQUID

PREP + COOK TIME 30 MINUTES **SERVES** 4

1kg (2 pounds) small whole squid, or 600g (1¼ pounds) cleaned squid

vegetable oil, for deep-frying

1½ tablespoons sea salt flakes, crushed lightly

2 teaspoons coarsely ground black pepper

3 teaspoons ground sichuan pepper

1 teaspoon chilli powder

⅔ cup (100g) cornflour (cornstarch)

4 long fresh red chillies, seeded, sliced thinly

1 green onion (scallion), sliced thinly

2 medium lemons (280g), halved or cut into wedges

1 Clean squid by gently pulling head and tentacles away from the body. Pull out the clear backbone and remove the entrails. Cut tentacles away from head just below the eyes; discard head. Discard hard beak in centre of tentacles. Cut tentacles in half, or quarters if large. Remove side wings and rub membrane from the body. Rinse body, tentacles and wings thoroughly; pat dry with paper towel. Cut the squid hoods down one side; open out and pat dry. Score the inside lightly with a small sharp knife in a criss-cross pattern, without cutting all the way through. Cut squid into 2.5cm x 5cm (1-inch x 2-inch) pieces. Pat dry with paper towel. (See also Seafood Techniques page 111.)

2 Heat oil in a wok or large saucepan to 180°C/350°F, or until surface starts to shimmer.

3 Meanwhile, combine salt, peppers and chilli powder in a medium bowl; reserve 2 teaspoons spice mixture. Stir cornflour into remaining spice mixture. Add squid, in batches, tossing to coat. Shake off any excess flour mixture. Transfer to a plate.

4 Deep-fry sliced chilli and green onion for 1 minute or until softened. Remove with a slotted spoon; drain on paper towel.

5 Deep-fry squid, in batches, for 1 minute, or until just tender and golden. Remove with a slotted spoon; drain well on paper towel.

6 Transfer squid to bowls; sprinkle with chilli mixture and reserved spice mixture. Serve with lemon halves.

JERK FISH TACOS

PREP + COOK TIME 30 MINUTES **SERVES** 8

Jerk is both the name for a Jamaican dry or wet spice seasoning, characterised by allspice and chillies, and the method of cooking over barbecue coals. Traditionally the seasoning is rubbed over chicken, pork and fish.

1 teaspoon ground allspice

½ teaspoon dried thyme

1½ teaspoons cayenne pepper

1 teaspoon ground cinnamon

1½ tablespoons garlic powder

2 teaspoons brown sugar

¼ cup (60ml) olive oil

800g (1½ pounds) firm white skinless fish fillets, cut into long pieces (see tips)

16 small (14cm) flour tortillas

avocado cream

2 medium avocados (500g)

½ cup (120g) sour cream

2 tablespoons lime juice

slaw

350g (11 ounces) white cabbage, shredded

2 cups loosely packed fresh coriander (cilantro) leaves

1 small red onion (100g), halved, sliced thinly

1 fresh long green chilli, seeded, sliced thinly

1 Combine allspice, thyme, cayenne pepper, cinnamon, garlic powder, sugar and oil in a medium bowl, add fish; toss gently to coat. Season with salt. Cover; refrigerate until required.

2 Make avocado cream and slaw.

3 Heat a large, non-stick frying pan over medium heat; heat tortillas, in batches, for 15 seconds each side. Wrap tortillas in foil to keep warm.

4 Increase heat to high; cook fish in same pan, in two batches, for 4 minutes or until just cooked.

5 Serve warm tortillas filled with slaw and fish, topped with avocado cream.

avocado cream Blend or process ingredients until smooth. Season to taste.

slaw Place ingredients in a large bowl; toss to combine. Season to taste.

tips Cut the fish fillets lengthways on the diagonal into 1.5cm (¾-inch) wide, 12cm (4¾-inch) long strips. The fish can be prepared 4 hours ahead to the end of step 1. Avocado cream and slaw can also be prepared up to 4 hours ahead; refrigerate until required.

PAN FRYING FISH

- Suitable fillets: snapper, whiting, bream, john dory and barramundi.
- Lightly dust thinner fillets in flour to protect the flesh and give it a crisp coating.
- Pan-fry in a little heated butter or olive oil, or a combination of both – just enough to cover the base of the frying pan.
- If the fish has skin, sprinkle with sea salt flakes and only flour the flesh side; cook skin-side down first, turn once to complete the cooking.
- If the fish has no skin, cook it on one side until lightly browned underneath, then turn and cook for a few more minutes until done.
- For thicker fillets, such as blue-eye, salmon or swordfish, pan-fry in a little olive oil over medium heat. Take the fish off the heat when it turns opaque or insert a fork into one fillet; if the flesh separates into flakes, it is done.

PRAWN FLAVOURS

Shell and devein 1kg (2 pounds) uncooked medium prawns (shrimp), leaving tails intact. Combine prawns with one of the flavours below, use immediately or refrigerate, covered, for 30 minutes. Cook prawns on an oiled heated chargrill pan or barbecue for 1 minute each side or until cooked through. Serves 4.

RED CURRY PRAWNS

Whisk ⅓ cup thai red curry paste with 1 cup (250ml) coconut milk until smooth and well combined. Toss prepared prawns with 1 cup marinade. Serve cooked prawns drizzled with remaining marinade and lime wedges.

HERB & CHILLI PRAWNS

Process 2 cups fresh mint leaves and 1 cup each fresh flat-leaf parsley leaves and coriander (cilantro) leaves until finely chopped. Add ½ cup olive oil, 1 teaspoon dried chilli flakes and 1 tablespoon red wine vinegar. Toss prepared prawns with ⅔ cup marinade. Serve cooked prawns with remaining marinade.

MALAYSIAN CURRY PRAWNS

Process 1 teaspoon chinese five spice powder with 2 fresh small red chillies, 2 cloves garlic, 3 shallots, 1 teaspoon grated ginger, 2 tablespoons tamarind paste, 1 teaspoon curry powder and ¼ cup coconut oil until smooth. Toss prepared prawns with marinade.

PASTA

COOKING PERFECT PASTA

To cook perfect pasta, bring a large saucepan of water to a rolling boil, add a few teaspoons salt, then pasta. To prevent pasta sticking, don't be tempted to add oil to the water, it will be wasted as it is drained away at the end, instead immediately stir the pasta for a few minutes. Dried pasta takes from 8-11 minutes to cook, use the packet instructions as a guide. However, always set your timer slightly earlier than the time given and scoop out a piece to test. It should be what the Italians call al dente, that is, firm to the bite. Fresh pasta will cook in 1-2 minutes.

AFTER COOKING

Once pasta is cooked, if it is to be used immediately, drain it over a bowl to collect the cooking water. The reserved cooking water, which contains some of the starch from the pasta can be used to thin thick pasta sauces like pesto. If the pasta is to be used later, it is advisable to undercook it if it is to be reheated; drain, cool under cold water then toss pasta with a generous amount of olive oil. Refrigerate pasta until needed, up to 1 day. To reheat, add pasta to a saucepan of boiling water and cook until heat through. Drain.

ROLLING CANNELLONI

Fresh cannelloni sheets are a lot easier to fill than dried cannelloni tubes. You can also use fresh lasagne sheets cut into shorter lengths if you are unable to find cannelloni sheets. Place a sheet lengthways on a work surface, with the short side in front of you. Spoon the filling 3cm (1¼ inches) up from the bottom edge, across the sheet in a neat line, so that the filling finishes at the halfway mark. Roll up from the end closest to you, place cannelloni seam-side down in the baking dish.

FRESH PAPPARDELLE

Pappardelle, one of the widest of the long pasta shapes, is traditionally served with meat sauces, such as bolognese sauce (see Beef Bolognese Lasagne, page 152). Dried pappardelle can be hard to find, which is why it is useful to know how to make a cheat's version from fresh lasagne sheets. Start by rolling up each lasagne sheet widthways, one at a time, then cut into 3cm (1¼-inch) wide strips. Once you've cut all the lasagne sheets, unfurl each roll. Fresh pasta will cook in around 1 minute, add to the boiling water and test a piece as soon as the water returns to the boil.

SPAGHETTI WITH GARLIC & OIL

PREP + COOK TIME 15 MINUTES **SERVES** 4

500g (1 pound) spaghetti • ⅓ cup (80ml) olive oil •
3 cloves garlic, sliced thinly • 2 tablespoons finely
chopped fresh flat-leaf parsley

Cook pasta in a large saucepan of boiling salted
water until almost tender; drain, reserving some of
the cooking water, if needed. Meanwhile, heat oil in
a large frying pan; cook garlic, gently, until golden.
Stir in parsley. Combine garlic mixture with pasta.
Serve as is, or make one of the variations, opposite.

146

ZUCCHINI & MINT

Make Spaghetti with Garlic & Oil (left), removing garlic from oil; reserve. Add 2 large coarsely grated zucchini to the frying pan with the garlic oil; cook, stirring, until just softened. Season. Add 2 tablespoons torn fresh mint, 1 teaspoon finely grated lemon rind and the pasta; toss to combine. Serve topped with 100g (3oz) crumbled persian fetta and reserved crisp garlic.

TUNA, ROCKET & CHILLI

Make Spaghetti with Garlic & Oil (left), adding 2 fresh seeded and chopped long red chillies, and 2 x 125g (4oz) canned drained tuna slices to the frying pan with the garlic. Add 125g (4oz) coarsely chopped rocket (arugula) and the pasta; season with salt and freshly ground black pepper, toss gently to combine. Serve with lemon cheeks.

FRESH TOMATO SAUCE

Make Spaghetti with Garlic & Oil (left) omitting the flat-leaf parsley. Halve 6 medium (1kg) ripe tomatoes; squeeze juice and seeds into a bowl. Coarsely chop tomato flesh; add to the bowl with ¼ cup baby capers and ⅓ cup lightly packed fresh basil leaves. Season. Toss tomato mixture through pasta with 100g (3oz) drained, torn baby bocconcini. Serve at room temperature.

GARLIC PRAWNS

Shell and devein 750g (1½lbs) uncooked prawns (shrimp), leaving tails intact. Make Spaghetti with Garlic & Oil (left), heating 1 tablespoon of the oil in a frying pan; cook prawns, tossing, for 1½ minutes or until cooked. Remove from pan. Heat remaining oil, add 2 small seeded sliced red chillies with the garlic. Return prawns to pan, with pasta and parsley; toss to combine.

CLASSIC PASTA & SAUCES

For these sauces, cook 400g (12½ ounces) of the pasta specified in the recipes below in a large saucepan of boiling water until just tender. Drain, reserving ½ cup cooking water (use as directed).

SPAGHETTI VONGOLE

PREP + COOK TIME 30 MINUTES (+ STANDING) **SERVES** 4

Soak 1kg (2lbs) vongole (clams) in cold water for 15 minutes (this will rid the vongole of sand); drain. Heat 2 tablespoons extra virgin olive oil in a large saucepan; cook 3 cloves crushed garlic and 1 thinly sliced fresh long red chilli, stirring, 1 minute. Add 1 tablespoon capers, 2 tablespoons lemon juice and 1 cup (250ml) dry white wine; bring to the boil. Add vongole; cook, covered, for 5 minutes or until vongole open (discard any that do not). Add cooked spaghetti and ½ cup finely chopped fresh flat-leaf parsley; toss gently to combine.

ORECCHIETTE PANGRATTATO

PREP + COOK TIME 40 MINUTES (+ STANDING) **SERVES** 4

Heat ⅓ cup olive oil in a large frying pan over medium heat; cook 1 cup breadcrumbs (made from stale bread, see General Techniques page 229) and 1 teaspoon each dried chilli flakes and sea salt flakes, stirring, for 5 minutes or until crumbs are golden. Add 4 thinly sliced cloves garlic; stir a further 3 minutes or until cooked. Add cooked orecchietti or penne, ½ cup reserved pasta cooking water, 2 tablespoons lemon juice, 2 teaspoon zested lemon rind (see General Techniques page 228) and ½ cup finely chopped fresh flat-leaf parsley; toss gently to combine. Season.

FETTUCCINE CARBONARA

PREP + COOK TIME 25 MINUTES **SERVES** 4

Cook 100g (3oz) thinly sliced torn pancetta or 4 finely chopped rindless bacon slices (260g) in a medium frying pan for 5 minutes or until starting to crisp. Add 2 thinly sliced cloves garlic; cook, stirring, 1 minute. Combine 4 lightly beaten eggs and ¾ cup (60g) finely grated parmesan in a medium bowl. Add pancetta mixture, egg mixture and ¼ cup reserved pasta cooking water to drained cooked fettuccine in pan; stir over medium heat 1 minute or until well combined. Be careful not to overcook or the egg will scramble. Season with pepper and serve with extra parmesan.

CASARECCE & PESTO

PREP + COOK TIME 25 MINUTES **SERVES** 4

Blend or process 2 chopped cloves garlic, ⅓ cup (50g) toasted pine nuts, ½ cup (40g) finely grated parmesan and 2 cups firmly packed fresh basil leaves until almost smooth. Gradually add ½ cup (125ml) extra virgin olive oil in a thin, steady stream, processing until combined. Combine pesto with cooked casarecce, penne or fussili and ¼ cup reserved pasta cooking water. Serve topped with extra pine nuts and fresh small basil leaves.
tip Pesto keeps, in an airtight container, covered with a thin layer of olive oil in the fridge for up to 1 week; freeze for up to 1 month.

GREEK-STYLE WHITE SAUCE

Make white sauce on page 152, using 3½ cups milk and 1½ cups greek-style yoghurt. Add 100g (3oz) crumbled fetta and ¼ teaspoon freshly grated or ground nutmeg to cooked sauce. Pair with the spiced lamb bolognese sauce (below) and pasta sheets for a lasagne or layer with grilled eggplant.

SALAMI CHILLI BOLOGNESE SAUCE

Make bolognese sauce on page 152. Stir in 100g (3oz) thinly sliced sopressa salami, 1 teaspoon fennel seeds, 2 finely chopped small red chillies and 2 tablespoons oregano leaves at the end of cooking. Pair with the spinach white sauce (below) and pasta sheets for a lasagne.

SPICED LAMB BOLOGNESE SAUCE

Make bolognese sauce on page 152 using minced lamb instead of beef, and adding 1½ teaspoons ground cumin and 1 cinnamon stick. Stir in ½ cup fresh coriander (cilantro) leaves at the end. Pair with greek-style white sauce (above) and pasta sheets for a lasagne or serve as sauce on pasta.

SPINACH WHITE SAUCE

Make white sauce on page 152. Add 100g (3oz) baby spinach leaves to a pan of boiling water; drain, cool under running water. Squeeze out excess water. Stir into sauce with ½ cup mascarpone and 2 teaspoons zested lemon rind. Pair with salami chilli bolognese sauce (above) and pasta sheets for lasagne.

BEEF BOLOGNESE LASAGNE

PREP + COOK TIME 2 HOURS (+ STANDING) **SERVES** 8

Bolognese, the most well-known and versatile of pasta sauces, can be served with spaghetti or layered between sheets of pasta for a classic lasagne. Or mix and match the bolognese sauce and white sauce with the variations on page 151 for a very modern lasagne.

500g (1 pound) fresh lasagne pasta sheets

2 cups (160g) finely grated parmesan

bolognese sauce

2 teaspoons olive oil

1 medium brown onion (150g), chopped finely

1 trimmed celery stalk (100g), chopped finely

600g (1¼ pounds) minced (ground) beef

2 cloves garlic, crushed

¼ cup (70g) tomato paste

800g (1½ pounds) canned crushed tomatoes

1 medium carrot (120g), grated finely

1 teaspoon dried oregano leaves

1½ cups (375ml) beef stock

½ cup coarsely chopped fresh flat-leaf parsley or basil

white sauce

125g (4 ounces) butter

¾ cup (110g) plain (all-purpose) flour

1.25 litres (5 cups) hot milk

1 Make bolognese sauce.

2 Preheat oven to 200°C/400°F. Grease a deep 25cm x 35cm (10-inch x 14-inch) baking dish.

3 Make white sauce.

4 Spread ½ cup of the white sauce over base of dish. Top with a layer of pasta sheets, a third of the bolognese sauce, ½ cup of the parmesan and 1 cup of the remaining white sauce in dish. Repeat layering two more times, starting with pasta sheets and ending with white sauce. Top lasagne with remaining cheese.

5 Bake lasagne for 40 minutes or until top is browned lightly. Stand 15 minutes before cutting.

bolognese sauce Heat oil in large heavy-based frying pan over medium heat; cook onion and celery, stirring, for 10 minutes or until vegetables soften. Add beef; cook, breaking up the lumps with a wooden spoon and stirring occasionally, until beef changes colour. Add garlic and tomato paste; cook, stirring, 1 minute. Stir in tomatoes and carrot then oregano and stock; bring to the boil. Reduce heat; simmer, uncovered, for 10 minutes or until thickened slightly. Stir in parsley.

white sauce Melt butter in a medium saucepan, add flour; stir until mixture forms a smooth paste. Gradually whisk in milk; bring to the boil, whisking, until sauce boils and thickens. Cool.

tips For extra richness try a combination of pork and veal mince, rather than just beef mince. Store bolognese sauce, covered, in the fridge for up to 3 days or freeze portions in airtight containers for up to 3 months.

SPINACH & RICOTTA CANNELLONI

PREP + COOK TIME 1 HOUR **SERVES** 6

750g (1½ pounds) baby spinach leaves, washed

500g (1 pound) firm ricotta

2 eggs

¼ cup finely chopped fresh mint

1 tablespoon fresh lemon thyme

1 tablespoon finely grated lemon rind

1½ cups (120g) coarsely grated parmesan

250g (8 ounces) fresh cannelloni sheets (see tip)

fresh basil leaves and lemon rind curls, to serve

tomato sauce

1 tablespoon olive oil

1 medium onion (150g), chopped finely

4 cloves garlic, crushed

½ cup (125ml) dry white wine

800g (1½ pounds) canned diced tomatoes

1 teaspoon caster (superfine) sugar

1 Make tomato sauce.

2 Meanwhile, preheat oven to 180°C/350°F.

3 Cook just washed and wet spinach in heated large saucepan, stirring, until wilted. Drain; when cool enough to handle, squeeze out excess moisture. Place spinach in a large bowl with ricotta, eggs, herbs, rind and ½ cup of the parmesan; stir until combined.

4 Spread a third of the tomato sauce on the base of a shallow 25cm x 35cm (10-inch x 14-inch) ovenproof dish.

5 Place 12 cannelloni sheets on a work surface, with the short side in front of you. Spoon filling on each sheet, starting 3cm (1¼ inches) up from the edge, across the sheet so that it finishes at the halfway mark (see Pasta Techniques page 145). Roll up cannelloni; place seam-side down, in single layer, on sauce in dish until dish is filled. Top with remaining sauce.

6 Cover dish with foil; bake for 20 minutes. Remove foil, sprinkle with remaining parmesan; bake for 15 minutes or until pasta is tender and parmesan is browned lightly.

tomato sauce Heat oil in a large saucepan; cook onion, stirring, until softened. Add garlic; cook, stirring, until fragrant. Add wine and tomatoes; bring to the boil. Reduce heat; simmer, uncovered, stirring occasionally, 20 minutes or until thickened slightly. Cool 10 minutes; blend or process sauce with sugar until smooth.

tip We used 12 cannelloni sheets; if they are not available, use 4 fresh pasta sheets and cut each sheet into thirds.

POTATO GNOCCHI WITH GARLIC & THYME

RECIPE PAGE 162

BEETROOT GNOCCHI

Finely grate 150g (4½oz) beetroot (beets). Heat 1 tablespoon olive oil in a small frying pan; cook beetroot, stirring, for 10 minutes or until soft. Puree in a small food processor. Make Potato Gnocchi (page 162), combining beetroot puree and mashed potato in step 2; add remaining ingredients.

KUMARA GNOCCHI

Finely grate 175g (5½oz) kumara. Heat 1 tablespoon olive oil in a small frying pan; cook kumara, stirring, for 10 minutes or until soft. Puree in a small food processor. Make Potato Gnocchi (page 162), combining kumara puree and mashed potato in step 2; add remaining ingredients.

KALE GNOCCHI

Finely shred 100g (3oz) baby kale leaves. Heat 1 tablespoon olive oil in a small frying pan; cook kale, stirring, for 5 minutes or until soft. Leave to cool. Make Potato Gnocchi (page 162), combining kale and mashed potato in step 2; add remaining ingredients.

PARSNIP GNOCCHI

Finely grate 175g (5½oz) parsnip. Heat 1 tablespoon olive oil in a small frying pan; cook parsnip and 1 teaspoon caraway seeds, stirring, for 10 minutes or until soft. Puree in a small food processor. Make Potato Gnocchi (page 162), combining parsnip and mashed potato in step 2; add remaining ingredients.

POTATO GNOCCHI WITH GARLIC & THYME

PREP + COOK TIME 1 HOUR (+ REFRIGERATION) **SERVES** 4

500g (1 pound) evenly sized desiree potatoes, unpeeled (see tip)

1 egg, beaten lightly with a pinch of salt

2 tablespoons finely grated parmesan

1 cup (150g) plain (all-purpose) flour, approximately

½ cup (40g) flaked parmesan

2 teaspoons fresh lemon thyme sprigs

butter sauce

¼ cup (60ml) olive oil

4 cloves garlic, sliced thinly

150g (4½ ounces) butter, chopped

1 tablespoon fresh lemon thyme leaves

1 Boil whole potatoes until tender; drain. When cool enough to handle, peel away skins.

2 Mash potatoes, using a ricer or potato masher into a medium bowl. Stir in egg, parmesan and ½ cup of the flour to make a firm dough (add a little more flour if the mixture is sticky).

3 Divide dough into four portions; roll each portion on a floured surface into long ropes, about 2cm (¾-inch) thick. Cut each rope into 2.5cm (1-inch) pieces.

4 Roll pieces into a ball then run each piece of dough over the back of a fork over the tines to create light indents (this will help the butter sauce cling to the gnocchi). Place gnocchi, in a single layer, on a lightly floured tray. Cover; refrigerate 1 hour.

5 Cook gnocchi, in batches, in a large saucepan of boiling salted water until gnocchi float to the surface and are cooked through. Remove from pan with a slotted spoon to a large shallow bowl; cover to keep warm.

6 When the last batch of gnocchi are in, start the butter sauce. Heat olive oil in a medium frying pan over medium heat, add garlic; cook, stirring, for 3 minutes or until golden. Remove with a slotted spoon. Add butter to the oil in the pan; cook swirling the pan occassionally for 2 minutes or until foamy and butter is nut brown in colour. Immediately remove from heat, add thyme.

7 Divide gnocchi among serving bowls, spoon over butter sauce; top with fried garlic, flaked parmesan and thyme sprigs. Season with freshly ground black pepper.

tip It is important to use the right type of potato for gnocchi as varieties vary in their moisture content. Choose a dry variety and cook them whole in their skins to minimise introducing any extra water.

COOKING POTATOES

Boil whole, unpeeled potatoes in a large saucepan. Drain; leave to cool. When potatoes are cool enough to handle, peel away the skin with a small knife. Use a dry variety of potato and cook them whole with the skin on to minimise introducing extra water.

MASHING POTATOES

If you have one, push the potatoes through a ricer into a medium bowl. A ricer is ideal for making super smooth mash. Otherwise, use a traditional potato masher until as smooth as possible or push the potatoes through a sieve.

MAKING GNOCCHI DOUGH

Combine mashed potato with egg, parmesan and half the flour until mixture forms a firm dough. Bring the mixture together on a lightly floured surface, adding a little more of the remaining flour until the dough is smooth and loses its stickiness.

CUTTING GNOCCHI DOUGH

Divide the gnocchi dough into four portions. On a lightly floured surface, roll one portion of dough with your fingers into a long rope about 2cm (¾-inch) thick. With a small knife, cut each long rope into 2.5cm (1-inch) pieces. Repeat with remaining ropes.

CREATING GNOCCHI SHAPES

Lightly roll each piece of gnocchi dough into a ball. Run each ball down the back of a fork over the tines to create light indents (these indents help the sauce cling to the gnocchi). Place gnocchi, in a single layer, on a floured tray. Cover; refrigerate for 1 hour.

COOKING GNOCCHI

Bring a large saucepan of salted water to the boil. Working in batches, add gnocchi to the boiling water. Gnocchi are cooked when they float to the surface. Use a slotted spoon to transfer gnocchi to a bowl, allowing the water to drain. Cover to keep warm.

MACARONI CHEESE

PREP + COOK TIME 1 HOUR **SERVES** 4

280g (9 ounces) macaroni pasta • 4 rindless bacon slices (260g), chopped finely • 50g (1½ ounces) butter • ⅓ cup (50g) plain (all-purpose) flour • 1 litre (4 cups) milk • 1 cup (120g) coarsely grated cheddar • ½ cup (40g) finely grated pecorino cheese • 2 tablespoons wholegrain mustard • ½ cup (35g) stale breadcrumbs

Preheat oven to 180°C/350°F. Oil a deep 2-litre (8-cup) ovenproof dish. Cook pasta in a large saucepan of boiling water for 1½ minutes less then cooking time on the packet; drain. Cook bacon in same pan, stirring, until crisp; drain on paper towel. Melt butter in same pan, add flour; cook, stirring, 1 minute. Gradually stir in milk; cook, stirring, until sauce boils and thickens. Stir in cheeses and mustard. Combine pasta, cheese sauce and bacon in a large bowl; pour into ovenproof dish. Top with breadcrumbs, dot with a little extra butter. Bake for 30 minutes or until browned.

FRIED RICE

Fried rice is best made with day-old cooked rice that has had a chance to chill and firm, otherwise the intense heat of the wok will make the rice mushy. Drier, firmer rice will keep its shape. Boil long-grain white rice or jasmine rice, or cook the rice following the absorption method on page 168. Drain if boiling the rice but don't rinse it; spread out immediately on a tray to cool slightly, then refrigerate until chilled. Don't leave cooked rice unrefrigerated.

GRAINS

Whole grains like barley, farro and green wheat freekeh are complex carbohydrates providing long lasting energy. Pearl barley has had the husk removed and has been steamed and polished for faster cooking. Farro, a cousin of wheat and spelt, like barley has a robust nutty flavour – both are boiled for about 45 minutes. Green wheat freekeh, a variety of wheat that is picked while it's still green and roasted, contains more nutrients than regular wheat. It is sold in a wholegrain form which takes 35 minutes to cook, and in cracked form which cooks in 15 minutes.

BASIC HUMMUS

PREP + COOK TIME 1¼ HOURS (+ SOAKING) **MAKES** 3 CUPS

1 cup (200g) dried chickpeas • 1 clove garlic, crushed •
¼ cup tahini • ¼ cup lemon juice • ¼ cup olive oil

Soak chickpeas in cold water overnight. Drain. Place drained
chickpeas in a large saucepan with plenty of water. Bring to a
simmer over high heat; simmer, uncovered, for 1 hour or until
tender. Drain, reserving ½ cup cooking water and ¼ cup whole
chickpeas. Process remaining chickpeas and reserved cooking
water until smooth. Add garlic, tahini, juice and oil. Season. Serve
topped with reserved chickpeas, a little extra oil and pitta bread.
tip Use 800g (1½ pounds) canned chickpeas instead of dried;
drain, reserving ½ cup liquid. Use only if needed to thin hummus.

170

GREEN HUMMUS

Make Basic Hummus (left) without reserving any whole chickpeas. Add ½ cup each firmly packed fresh coriander (cilantro) leaves and fresh mint leaves; process hummus mixture until smooth. Serve topped with ⅓ cup crumbled fetta and extra fresh coriander and mint leaves. Drizzle with a little extra olive oil.

CARROT HUMMUS

Make Basic Hummus (left) without reserving any whole chickpeas. Heat 2 tablespoons olive oil in a frying pan over medium heat; cook 1½ cups coarsely grated carrot and ¾ teaspoon each crushed coriander seeds and ground turmeric, stirring, for 8 minutes until soft. Add carrot mixture to hummus; process until smooth. Serve sprinkled with sumac, drizzle with oil.

SEED & SPICE HUMMUS

Make Basic Hummus (left) without reserving any whole chickpeas. Heat 2 tablespoons olive oil in a small frying pan over medium heat; cook 2 tablespoons pepitas (pumpkin seeds), and 1 teaspoon each cumin, sesame seeds and crushed coriander seeds, stirring, for 3 minutes or until toasted. Serve drizzled with extra oil; top with spice mixture and strips of lemon rind.

HUMMUS WITH POMEGRANATE LAMB

Make Basic Hummus (left) without reserving whole chickpeas. Heat 2 tablespoons olive oil in frying pan over high heat; cook 200g (6oz) minced lamb, 1 crushed clove garlic, 2 tablespoons pomegranate molasses and ½ teaspoon allspice, stirring, 15 minutes or until lamb is almost crisp. Serve topped with lamb mixture, 2 tablespoons pomegranate seeds and coriander.

CHICKEN & CHORIZO PAELLA

PREP + COOK TIME 1 HOUR   **SERVES** 6

large pinch saffron threads

¼ cup (60ml) boiling water

600g (1¼ pounds) uncooked medium king prawns (shrimp)

1kg (2 pounds) black mussels

1 tablespoon olive oil

600g (1¼ pounds) chicken thigh fillets, chopped coarsely

300g (9½ ounces) chorizo, sliced thinly

1 large red onion (300g), chopped finely

1 large red capsicum (bell pepper) (300g), chopped finely

3 cloves garlic, chopped

2 teaspoons smoked paprika

250g (8 ounces) grape tomatoes

1½ cups (300g) calasparra rice or arborio rice

3 cups (750ml) chicken stock

250g (4 ounces) green beans, halved lengthways

2 tablespoons chopped fresh flat-leaf parsley

lemon wedges and alioli, to serve

1 Place saffron and boiling water in a small bowl. Stand for 15 minutes.

2 Meanwhile, shell and devein prawns, leaving the tails intact. Scrub mussels and remove the beards. (See Seafood Techniques pages 110 & 111.)

3 Heat oil in a 38cm (15¼-inch) (top measurement) paella pan or very large frying pan; cook chicken until browned both sides. Remove from pan. Add chorizo to same pan; cook until browned on both sides. Remove from pan.

4 Add onion, capsicum, garlic and paprika to same pan; cook, stirring, until soft. Stir in tomatoes. Add rice; stir to coat in the mixture.

5 Return chicken and chorizo to pan with stock and saffron mixture; stir only until combined. Season. Do not stir again. Bring to boil, then simmer, uncovered, for 15 minutes or until the rice is almost tender.

6 Place beans over rice. Place prawns and mussels evenly over the surface of paella. Cover pan with large sheets of foil; cook, covered, for 5 minutes or until prawns are just cooked through and mussels have opened. (The cooking time will depend on the evenness of the heat under the pan. It is useful to rotate the pan during cooking so the heat is distributed evenly.) Sprinkle with parsley. Serve paella immediately with lemon wedges and alioli.

tips The best type of rice to use for paella is calasparra, a Spanish short grain rice available from delis and speciality food stores. A perfect paella should have a delicious golden crust on the bottom and the rice should have absorbed all the moisture.

BASIC RISOTTO

PREP + COOK TIME 35 MINUTES **SERVES** 4

1.5 litres (6 cups) chicken stock · 100g (3 ounces) butter, chopped ·
1 medium brown onion (150g), chopped finely · 2 cloves garlic, crushed ·
2 cups (400g) carnaroli or arborio rice · ½ cup (125ml) dry white wine ·
1 cup (80g) grated parmesan

Bring stock to a simmer in a medium saucepan; keep warm on low heat.
Heat half the butter in a heavy-based saucepan over medium heat; cook
onion and garlic, stirring, for 5 minutes or until onion is soft. Add rice; stir
for 2 minutes or until well coated. Add wine; bring to the boil. Stir in 1 cup
hot stock until absorbed. Continue adding stock mixture, 1 cup at a time,
stirring frequently, until absorbed after each addition. Stir in remaining
butter and parmesan. Serve as is, or use one of the variations, opposite.

PRAWN & ASPARAGUS RISOTTO

Shell and devein 500g (1lb) uncooked medium prawns (shrimp), leaving 12 with tails intact. Make Basic Risotto (left). Heat 2 tablespoons olive oil and 30g (1oz) butter in frying pan over medium heat; cook prawns, 340g (11oz) trimmed asparagus and 2 cloves crushed garlic, stirring, until prawns change colour. Stir prawn mixture into risotto; sprinkle with chilli flakes.

MUSHROOM & THYME RISOTTO

Make Basic Risotto (left). Using 90g (3oz) butter, cook 350g (11oz) mixed mushrooms (enoki, oyster and button mushrooms) and 2 tablespoons lemon thyme, in three batches, in a frying pan over medium-high heat until browned and tender. Stir half the mushroom mixture into risotto; top with remaining mushroom mixture, grated parmesan and extra lemon thyme.

PANCETTA, PEA & CHERVIL RISOTTO

Make Basic Risotto (left). Preheat grill (broiler). Place 4 slices round pancetta or prosciutto on an oven tray; cook under the grill for 4 minutes or until browned and crisp. Just before serving, stir ¾ cup thawed frozen peas into risotto until heated through. Serve topped with torn pancetta, grated parmesan and 2 tablespoons fresh chervil, basil or flat-leaf parsley leaves.

PUMPKIN & SAGE RISOTTO

Make Basic Risotto (left). Meanwhile, heat 2 tablespoons olive oil in a frying pan over medium heat; cook ½ cup loosely packed sage leaves, stirring, for 2 minutes or until crisp. Remove with a slotted spoon to paper towel. In the same pan, cook 500g (1lb) chopped pumpkin, turning until browned and tender. Just before serving, stir pumpkin and sage into risotto.

JEWELLED CHICKEN PILAF

PREP + COOK TIME 45 MINUTES **SERVES** 4

3 medium onions (510g), halved

3 cloves garlic, halved

2 teaspoons coarsely chopped ginger

1 teaspoon garam masala

1 teaspoon ground turmeric

½ teaspoon ground chilli

1½ tablespoons tomato paste

1 cup (280g) greek-style yoghurt

600g (1½ pounds) chicken thigh fillets, sliced thickly

90g (3 ounces) ghee (see tips) or vegetable oil

⅓ cup (55g) sultanas

⅓ cup (50g) pistachios

1½ cups (300g) basmati rice

1 cinnamon stick

8 cardamom pods, bruised

1½ cups (375ml) chicken stock

1½ cups (375ml) water

½ cup fresh coriander (cilantro) leaves

1 Process one of the halved onions with garlic and ginger until finely chopped. Add garam masala, turmeric, chilli, tomato paste and yoghurt; process to combine. Transfer marinade to a bowl. Add chicken; turn to coat. Cover; stand for 20 minutes.

2 Meanwhile, thinly slice remaining onions. Heat half the ghee in a medium frying pan over medium heat; cook sliced onions, stirring occasionally, for 20 minutes or until golden. Remove onion from pan with a slotted spoon, reserving as much ghee in the pan as possible. Add sultanas and pistachios to pan; cook, stirring, for 3 minutes or until nuts are toasted. Remove from pan, combine with onion mixture.

3 Scrape yoghurt marinade from chicken and reserve. Heat remaining ghee in same frying pan over medium heat; cook chicken, in two batches, for 2 minutes each side or until browned. Return all chicken to the pan. Add rice, reserved yoghurt mixture, cinnamon, cardamom, stock and the water; bring to the boil. Reduce heat; cook, covered, over low heat, for 15 minutes or until liquid is absorbed. Remove from heat; stand, covered, for 5 minutes. Serve pilaf topped with onion mixture and coriander.

tips If you like, you could use turkey steaks or boneless lamb leg, instead of the chicken; almonds instead of pistachios; and pomegranate seeds instead of sultanas, sprinkling them on the pilaf at the end of cooking. tip Ghee is clarified butter, meaning the milk solids have been removed. The lack of milk solids gives this fat a high smoking point so it can be heated to a high temperature without burning. It is available from most large supermarkets.

COOKING NOTES

Dried chinese pork sausages (lap cheong) and shrimp paste (belachan) are both sold in Asian grocers and the Asian section of most supermarkets. Nasi goreng, which translates as "fried rice" in Indonesia and Malaysia, was originally created to use leftover rice.

NASI GORENG

PREP + COOK TIME 40 MINUTES **SERVES** 4

720g (1½ pounds) cooked medium king prawns (shrimp)

2 tablespoons peanut oil

175g (5½ ounces) dried chinese sausages, sliced thickly

1 medium red capsicum (bell pepper) (200g), sliced

2 cloves garlic, crushed

2 teaspoons grated fresh ginger

1 teaspoon shrimp paste

2 fresh long red chillies, sliced thinly

4 cups (600g) cold cooked white long-grain rice (see tip)

2 tablespoons kecap manis

1 tablespoon light soy sauce

4 green onions (scallions), sliced thinly

4 eggs

1 Shell and devein prawns, leaving tails intact (see Seafood Techniques, page 110).

2 Heat a quarter of the oil in a wok over high heat; stir-fry sausage, in batches, until browned. Remove from wok.

3 Heat half the remaining oil in wok; stir-fry capsicum, garlic, ginger, paste and three-quarters of the chilli until softened. Add prawns and rice; stir-fry for 2 minutes. Return sausage to wok with sauces and half the green onion; stir-fry until combined.

4 Heat extra oil in a large frying pan over medium heat; fry eggs, one side only, until just set.

5 Divide nasi goreng between bowls, top with eggs; sprinkle with remaining green onion.

tip You will need to cook 2 cups (400g) white long-grain rice the day before making this recipe. Spread it in a thin layer on a tray and refrigerate it overnight. Alternatively you can use bought ready-cooked rice.

BASIC QUINOA

PREP + COOK TIME 20 MINUTES **SERVES** 4

1 cup (200g) quinoa (red, white or tri-coloured) •
2 cups (500ml) water

Rinse quinoa in a sieve under cold running water. Place
quinoa and the water in a medium saucepan; bring to the
boil. Reduce heat to low; cook, covered, for 15 minutes or
until quinoa is tender. Drain; cool slightly. Serve as is,
or in one of the salad variations, opposite.

QUINOA HALOUMI SALAD

Make Basic Quinoa (left). Combine 1 clove crushed garlic, 2 tablespoons each lemon juice and olive oil and 2 teaspoons each ground cumin and coriander. Add to quinoa with 100g (3oz) baby kale and ¼ cup mint leaves; toss. Cook 250g (8oz) sliced haloumi in an oiled frying pan over high heat, 1 minute each side until golden; top salad. Sprinkle with pomegranate seeds.

MOROCCAN CHICKEN QUINOA SALAD

Make Basic Quinoa (left). Heat 2 tablespoons oil in a small frying pan; cook 1 clove crushed garlic, 1 chopped red onion, 1½ teaspoons each ground ginger, cinnamon and turmeric, 8 minutes or until onion is soft. Add to quinoa with 500g (1lb) shredded chicken and ½ cup each halved sicilian olives and parsley, and 1 tablespoon each lemon juice and sliced preserved lemon rind.

QUINOA, LENTILS & SEEDS

Make Basic Quinoa (left); place in a bowl. Add 400g (12½oz) canned lentils, 425g (13½oz) mixed cherry tomatoes, 1 finely chopped small red onion, 2 tablespoons each toasted peptitas, sunflower seeds and pine nuts and ½ cup each currants, parsley and coriander leaves. Drizzle with 2 tablespoons each lemon juice and olive oil; toss. Top with fetta and toasted flaked almonds.

PUMPKIN & QUINOA SALAD

Make Basic Quinoa (left). Preheat oven to 200°C/425°F. Toss 1kg (2lb) jap pumpkin cut into wedges in 2 tablespoons olive oil on an oven tray; roast 30 minutes until tender. Combine 2 tablespoons each lime juice, fish sauce, brown sugar, peanut oil and coriander (cilantro) and 1 thinly sliced long red chilli. Combine quinoa, dressing and pumpkin; top with thai basil leaves.

CHILLI WHITE BEAN PANZANELLA

PREP + COOK TIME 20 MINUTES **SERVES** 4

160g (5 ounces) wholegrain sourdough bread

cooking oil spray

800g (1½ pounds) canned cannellini beans, drained, rinsed

250g (8 ounces) heirloom cherry tomatoes, halved

2 lebanese cucumbers (260g), chopped

1 small red onion (100g), sliced thinly

½ cup (60g) pitted sicilian olives, halved

1 fresh long red chilli, seeded, sliced thinly

1 cup loosely packed fresh basil leaves, torn

120g (4 ounces) soft goat's cheese, crumbled

¼ cup (60ml) olive oil

⅓ cup (80ml) red wine vinegar

1 clove garlic, crushed

1 Preheat oven to 220°C/425°F. Line a large oven tray with baking paper.

2 Roughly tear bread into pieces, place on tray; spray with cooking oil. Bake for 5 minutes or until golden and crisp.

3 Place bread in a large bowl with beans, tomatoes, cucumber, onion, olives, chilli, basil and half the cheese; toss gently to combine.

4 Combine oil, vinegar and garlic in a small bowl; season to taste. Spoon dressing over salad; top with remaining cheese. Serve immediately.

tips You can use marinated fetta instead of goat's cheese and black kalamata olives instead of green sicilian olives, if you like. This take on the traditional Italian salad panzanella, includes cannellini beans and cheese beefing up the nutritional content with protein, making it more of a main than a side salad. If you like, skip the cheese and stir through a can of flaked drained tuna.

STORING TIPS

This soup, without the seed topping, can be frozen for up to 3 months.

BARLEY & VEGETABLE SOUP WITH CRUNCHY SEEDS

PREP + COOK TIME 45 MINUTES **SERVES** 6

2 tablespoons extra virgin olive oil

1 large red onion (300g), chopped finely

1 medium parsnip (250g), chopped coarsely

2 stalks celery (300g), trimmed, chopped coarsely

4 cloves garlic, chopped finely

1 cup (250ml) bottled passata

1 litre (4 cups) vegetable stock

1 litre (4 cups) water

2 medium red capsicums (bell peppers) (400g), chopped coarsely

400g (12½ ounces) canned cannellini beans, drained, rinsed

½ cup (100g) pearl barley, rinsed

2 tablespoons pepitas (pumpkin seeds)

2 tablespoons sunflower seeds

¼ cup loosely packed torn fresh basil leaves

½ cup (40g) finely grated parmesan

1 Heat half the oil in a large saucepan over medium heat; cook onion, parsnip, celery and garlic, stirring, for 5 minutes or until vegetables have softened.

2 Add passata, stock and the water; bring to the boil. Stir in capsicum, beans and barley; simmer, covered, for 25 minutes or until barley is tender. Season to taste.

3 Meanwhile, heat remaining oil in a small frying pan over medium-high heat; cook seeds, stirring, until browned lightly and fragrant.

4 Just before serving, stir basil into soup. Ladle soup into bowls; sprinkle with seed mixture and parmesan.

tip The vegetables in this soup can be swapped with whatever you have on hand, just make sure that the substitute vegetable is the same weight as its replacement. Alternative vegetables include: carrots, potatoes, celeriac, orange sweet potato (kumara) and turnips. Green beans are also suitable, but should be added during the last 10 minutes of the cooking time.

CHICKPEA, FARRO, ORANGE & CHERRY SALAD

PREP + COOK TIME 45 MINUTES **SERVES** 4

1½ cups (300g) farro or barley

500g (1 pound) butternut pumpkin, cut into 1.5cm (¾-inch) pieces

1 tablespoon olive oil

2 teaspoons cumin seeds

2 medium oranges (480g)

400g (12½ ounces) canned chickpeas (garbanzo beans), drained, rinsed

⅓ cup (55g) almonds, roasted, chopped coarsely

¼ cup (35g) sunflower seeds, toasted lightly

300g (9½ ounces) cherries, halved, pitted

¼ cup chopped fresh mint

2 tablespoons torn fresh flat-leaf parsley

2 tablespoons pomegranate molasses

½ cup (125ml) extra virgin olive oil

2 tablespoon small fresh mint leaves, extra

1 Preheat oven to 220°C/425°F.

2 Cook farro in a large saucepan of boiling water for 35 minutes or until tender; drain. Rinse under cold water; drain well.

3 Meanwhile, combine pumpkin, olive oil and cumin seeds on a large oven tray; season. Bake for 20 minutes or until tender and beginning to brown around edges.

4 Remove rind from oranges with a zester, into long thin strips. Segment oranges over a bowl to catch the juices then squeeze the membrane (see General Techniques page 228); reserve 2 tablespoons of juice.

5 Place farro, pumpkin, orange segments and rind in a large bowl with chickpeas, almonds, sunflower seeds, cherries and herbs. Combine reserved orange juice, pomegranate molasses and extra virgin olive oil in a small jug. Drizzle dressing over salad, season to taste; toss to combine. Serve salad topped with extra mint.

tips This textural salad of grains, nuts and fruit can be eaten as a light lunch or serve it as a side dish with chicken or lamb. Grapes would make a nice alternative to the cherries.

COOKING NOTES

Farro is a grain related
to wheat with a similar
delicious nutty taste,
however unlike wheat and
spelt, which can take hours
to cook, it is relatively
fast-cooking. You will find
it in health food stores.

BASIC COUSCOUS

PREP + COOK TIME 10 MINUTES **SERVES** 4

1½ cups (300g) instant couscous • 20g (¾ ounce) butter, chopped • 1¼ cups (310ml) boiling water or chicken stock

Place couscous and butter in a medium heatproof bowl. Add the boiling water. Cover with plastic wrap; stand for 5 minutes. Fluff the couscous with a fork. Season to taste. Serve as is, or as one of the flavour variations, opposite.

LEMON & MINT COUSCOUS

Make Basic Couscous (left). Stir in 1 cup baby spinach leaves, the rind of 1 lemon zested into curls (see General Techniques page 228), 2 tablespoons lemon juice and 2 tablespoons extra virgin olive oil. Sprinkle with ¼ cup toasted natural flaked almonds and ¼ cup small fresh mint leaves.

CITRUS & FIG COUSCOUS

Make Basic Couscous (left). Add the finely grated rind, segments and juice from the membrane of 1 orange (see General Techniques page 228). Stir in 8 halved dried figs, 1 tablespoon thinly sliced preserved lemon rind and ¼ cup chopped fresh coriander (cilantro) and ¼ cup pistachios; season.

SPICY RED COUSCOUS

Make Basic Couscous (left). Heat 2 tablespoons olive oil in a saucepan; cook 2 teaspoons each harissa paste and smoked paprika, and 2 thinly sliced green onions (scallions), stirring, 2 minutes or until fragrant. Stir into couscous with 1 tablespoon red wine vinegar. Top with fetta and extra green onion.

OLIVE & PINE NUT COUSCOUS

Make Basic Couscous (left). Stir ½ cup pine nuts in a dry frying pan over medium heat for 3 minutes or until golden. Add to couscous with ½ cup halved green sicilian olives, 2 teaspoons finely grated lemon rind, ¼ cup lemon juice and ¼ cup small flat-leaf parsley leaves; stir to combine.

SOFT POLENTA

PREP + COOK TIME 30 MINUTES **SERVES** 4

Bring 1 litre (4 cups) stock, water or milk (or half stock and half milk) to the boil in a large deep saucepan. Add 1 cup (170g) polenta in a thin steady stream and whisk until the mixture comes to the boil. Reduce heat to low; cook, stirring, with a long-handled wooden spoon or whisk, for about 25 minutes until soft and thick. Stir in 30g (1 ounce) chopped butter and ½ cup (40g) grated parmesan. Season to taste. Adjust the consistency with a little extra milk if needed. Serve immediately.

COOKING NOTES

Polenta can also be barbecued or grilled.
Brush with a little olive oil and barbecue
or char-grill until browned and a crust
forms. Turn once and brown the other side.

CRISP POLENTA

PREP + COOK TIME 30 MINUTES (+ REFRIGERATION) **SERVES** 4

Grease a deep 20cm (8-inch) square cake pan; line base and sides
with baking paper. Make Soft Polenta (left), using instant polenta
and 3 cups stock; cook for 10 minutes. Pour mixture into pan. Cover;
refrigerate for 3 hours or until firm. Preheat oven to 220°C/425°F.
Line a large oven tray with baking paper. Remove polenta from pan;
cut into 20 chips. Place chips on tray; sprinkle with ¾ cup grated
parmesan, turn to coat all sides. Bake for 15 minutes or until
golden and crisp. Season with flaked salt.

VEGETABLES

SEEDING TOMATOES

While tomato seeds are edible they can interfere with the texture of a dish, especially if there are lots of them, as is the case with large tomato varieties. In some instances the seeds are also removed to reduce the moisture content in a recipe. To remove the seeds, cut the tomato in half horizontally, using a small serrated knife. Hold the tomato over a bowl and scoop out the seeds with a teaspoon. Chop or slice as specified in the recipe.

SEEDING CUCUMBERS

Like tomatoes, cucumber seeds are edible and increase the moisture of a recipe. For many salads this isn't a concern. For sauces, like tzatziki or raita that are combined with another wet ingredient, like yoghurt they are best removed. To remove seeds, cut the cucumber in half horizontally. Scoop along the length of the seeds with either a melon baller or teaspoon. To further reduce the water content, salt the cucumber lightly, turn cut-side down onto paper towel; stand 15 minutes, pat dry.

PUMPKIN TRICKS

Pumpkins are notoriously difficult to peel so current kitchen wisdom is to avoid peeling them when possible. Soft-skinned pumpkins such as jap, kent and golden nugget all have edible skins. Even with inedible skinned types, if you are cutting the pumpkin into large wedges for roasting the skin can be removed by the eater. Depending on the size of the pumpkin, cut it into 3cm (1¼-inch) wide wedges, or for smaller and elongated pumpkins into quarters or sixth, then remove the seeds with a spoon. The seeds can be roasted on a separate tray, drizzled with olive oil for about 15 minutes.

REFRESHING VEGETABLES

To cook green vegetables, such as asparagus, green beans, broccoli, sugar snap peas, peas and snow peas for a salad, or ahead of time, up to 4 hours, it is best to blanch them. Fill a large bowl with water, then add a couple of trays of ice-cubes. Bring a large saucepan of salted water to the boil. Cook each type of vegetable separately, and large quantities in batches, until just tender. (Green vegetables are nicest with a little bit of resistance when eaten.) Remove vegetables from water with a slotted spoon or with tongs for asparagus. Transfer to the bowl of ice water to stop cooking and cool. Drain when cooled; refrigerate until required.

JAPANESE GREEN BEANS

Snip 2 nori sheets into small pieces with scissors. Halve 500g (1lb) green beans lengthways; cook beans in a large saucepan of boiling water for 3 minutes. Drain. Dry pan. Heat 2 tablespoons olive oil in same pan; cook 2 thinly sliced green onions (scallions), stirring, 2 minutes. Return beans to pan; stir in 2 tablespoons toasted sesame seeds and the nori. Season.

BROCCOLINI & CRUMBS

Heat ⅓ cup olive oil in a frying pan over medium heat; stir ¾ cup panko (japanese) breadcrumbs and 1 teaspoon salt flakes 5 minutes or until golden. Add 4 cloves thinly sliced garlic; stir 3 minutes or until cooked. Add ¼ cup fresh flat-leaf parsley and 1 teaspoon grated lemon rind. Boil 460g (14½oz) trimmed broccolini 3 minutes until tender. Drain; toss with crumb mixture.

PEAS & PARMESAN CRUNCH

Finely grate 80g (2½oz) parmesan. Line a sandwich press with baking paper, spread with half the parmesan, cover with paper; close the lid, cook 3 minutes or until golden. Repeat with remaining parmesan. Boil 200g (6½oz) each sugar snap peas, snow peas and frozen peas, in batches, until just tender. Drain; toss with 1 tablespoon olive oil. Top with crumbled parmesan crunch.

ZUCCHINI & ALMONDS

Cut 6 small zucchini lengthways into four. Heat ⅓ cup olive oil in a frying pan over medium heat; cook zucchini, in two batches, for 3 minutes each side or until golden. Remove with tongs or a slotted spoon. Add ½ cup flaked natural almonds to pan; cook, stirring, 3 minutes or until golden. Return zucchini to pan; toss to combine. Season and serve with lemon cheeks.

SILVER BEET WITH PINE NUTS

Trim 6cm (2½-in) from stem ends 380g (12oz) silver beet (swiss chard); discard. Chop remaining silver beet coarsely, keeping leaves and white stem separate. Heat ¼ cup olive oil in a frying pan over medium heat; cook 1 large thinly sliced red onion, white stems and ⅓ cup raisins, stirring, for 5 minutes. Add leaves; stir 8 minutes or until tender. Stir in ½ cup toasted pine nuts.

CHAR-GRILLED ASPARAGUS

Trim 2cm (¾-in) from the ends 480g (15½oz) asparagus. Preheat a char-grill pan. Group asparagus in threes, side-by-side, then thread two toothpicks through each group to hold them together. Brush asparagus with 2 tablespoons each combined kecap manis and olive oil. Char-grill for 2 minutes each side. Serve with baby rocket and lime wedges.

CAVOLO NERO & MUSTARD SEEDS

Trim 5cm (2-in) from stem end of 190g (6oz) cavolo nero (tuscan cabbage); discard. Cut remainder of stems in half crossways. Heat 2 tablespoons olive oil in a frying pan over medium heat; cook 1 teaspoon brown mustard seeds and 1 clove crushed garlic, stirring, for 2 minutes. Add cavolo nero; cook, stirring, for 5 minutes or until wilted. Sprinkle with grated lemon rind.

BRUSSELS SPROUTS, DUKKAH & HONEY

Trim ends from 500g (1lb) brussels sprouts; cut in half. Place in a bowl with 2 tablespoons each honey and olive oil. Season with salt and pepper; toss well to combine. Heat a non-stick frying pan over medium heat; cook sprouts, cut-side down, for 2 minutes or until tender. Turn over; cook for 2 mintues or until tender. Add 2 tablespoons dukkah; toss to combine.

CAULIFLOWER 'FRIED RICE'

PREP + COOK TIME 30 MINUTES **SERVES** 4

½ medium cauliflower (700g), florets coarsely chopped, stems discarded

1½ tablespoons virgin coconut oil

2 free-range eggs, beaten lightly

2 teaspoons sesame oil

1 large carrot (180g), sliced thinly on the diagonal

1 medium red onion (170g), cut into thin wedges

½ teaspoon chinese five spice powder

300g (9½ ounces) broccolini, halved crossways

¼ cup (60ml) water

2 cloves garlic, crushed

1 tablespoon finely grated fresh ginger

2 green onions (scallions), sliced thinly

1 fresh long red chilli, sliced thinly (optional)

1 Pulse cauliflower in a food processor until cut into rice-sized pieces. Steam or microwave for 6 minutes or until just tender; season to taste.

2 Meanwhile, heat a wok on high heat; add 1 teaspoon of the coconut oil, swirl wok to coat with oil. Add egg; swirl wok to form a thin omelette. Cook until omelette is just set; transfer to a clean chopping board. Roll tightly; cut into thin strips.

3 Heat remaining coconut oil with sesame oil in wok; stir-fry carrot, red onion and five spice, for 4 minutes or until just tender. Add broccolini and the water; stir-fry for 2 minutes or until just tender. Add garlic, ginger and half the green onion; stir-fry until fragrant. Add cauliflower; stir-fry for 2 minutes or until heated through. Season to taste.

4 Serve cauliflower fried rice immediately, topped with omelette strips, remaining green onion and chilli, if using.

MIX IT UP

Other vegetables such as red cabbage and capsicum can be used instead of carrot and broccolini in this recipe with the cauliflower. You could also add some peas and beans. For a broccoli 'fried rice', simply use the same quantity of broccoli in place of the cauliflower and asparagus instead of broccolini.

ASIAN VEGETABLES

Asian vegetable are the unassuming stars of the vegetable world. Cheap to buy, fast to cook and easy to transform into tasty hot side dishes or crisp textural salads. Serve them with barbecued meats or skewers.

CHOY SUM & CRISP TOFU
PREP + COOK TIME 20 MINUTES **SERVES** 4

Cut 300g (9½oz) firm tofu into 2.5cm (1-in) cubes. Heat ¼ cup vegetable oil in a wok over medium heat. Fry tofu, in two batches, turning, for 6 minutes or until crisp; drain on paper towel. Trim ends from 450g (14½oz) choy sum, then cut in half. Drain all but 2 tablespoons oil from wok. Heat oil in wok over high heat; stir-fry 1 thinly sliced clove garlic and 4cm (1½-in) piece ginger cut into matchsticks, for 1 minute. Add choy sum stems; stir-fry 1 minute. Add choy sum leaves and 250g (8oz) halved cherry tomatoes; stir-fry 1 minute. Add tofu and 2 tablespoons tamari; toss to heat.

WOMBOK SALAD CRUNCH
PREP TIME 15 MINUTES **SERVES** 6

Coarsely chop ½ wombok (1kg). Cut 2 medium carrots into matchsticks with a mandoline or julienne peeler (see General Techniques page 228). Combine 1 tablespoon sesame oil, 1 tablespoon vegetable olive oil, ¼ cup rice wine vinegar, 1 clove crushed garlic and ½ small seeded finely chopped fresh red chilli in a small bowl. Heat 1½ tablespoons vegetable oil in a wok until almost smoking. Add wombok; toss for 1 minute or until slightly wilted. Remove from heat; stir in carrot, dressing, ½ cup fresh thai basil leaves and 2 tablespoons toasted sesame seeds.

GAI LAN & OYSTER SAUCE
PREP + COOK TIME 15 MINUTES **SERVES** 4

Place 4 thinly sliced cloves garlic and ¼ cup peanut oil in a wok over medium heat. Once oil starts to sizzle, stir garlic, 2 minutes or until golden; remove with a slotted spoon. Discard all but 1½ tablespoons oil from wok. Trim 600g (1¼lbs) gai lan; cut in half. Cook stems in a large pan of boiling water for 1 minute. Add leaves to pan; cook a further 30 seconds until leaves and stems are almost tender. Drain. Heat reserved oil in wok over high heat, add gai lan, ¼ cup oyster sauce and 2 tablespoons soy sauce; stir-fry for 2 minutes. Serve topped with garlic and thinly sliced red chilli.

SNAKE BEANS & RICE
PREP + COOK TIME 15 MINUTES **SERVES** 4

Cut 500g (1lb) snake beans into 10cm (4-in) lengths. Cook beans in a large saucepan of boiling water for 3 minutes or until tender; drain. Place 1½ tablespoons lime juice, 1 tablespoon each fish sauce, kecap manis and peanut oil, 2 teaspoons grated palm sugar and ½ finely chopped fresh red chilli in a screw-top jar; shake well. Heat 2 tablespoons peanut oil in a wok over medium heat, add 500g (1lb) ready-cooked packaged jasmine rice; stir-fry 3 minutes or until heated through. Add snake beans, ¼ cup finely chopped unsalted peanuts and dressing; toss well to combine.

DOUBLE CHEESE POTATO GRATIN

PREP + COOK TIME 1 HOUR 35 MINUTES (+ STANDING) **SERVES** 8

300ml pouring cream

1 cup (250ml) milk

50g (1½ ounces) butter

¼ teaspoon ground nutmeg

2 cloves garlic, bruised

3 sprigs fresh thyme

1.5kg (3 pounds) potatoes (see tips)

1 cup (120g) coarsely grated smoked cheddar

½ cup (40g) coarsely grated parmesan

sprigs fresh thyme, extra, to serve

1 Heat cream, milk, butter, nutmeg, garlic and thyme in medium saucepan until just below boiling point. Remove pan from heat; stand for 15 minutes. Discard garlic and thyme.

2 Meanwhile, preheat oven to 200°C/400°F. Grease a 2-litre (8-cup) shallow ovenproof dish.

3 Use a mandoline or V-slicer to slice potatoes thinly. Layer potato and cheddar in dish; pour cream mixture over the top. Cover dish with greased foil.

4 Bake gratin, covered, for 45 minutes. Remove foil; sprinkle gratin with parmesan. Bake, uncovered, for 20 minutes or until potato is tender and browned. Stand for 10 minutes before serving topped with extra thyme.

tips Use a floury variety of potato such as spunta, desiree or russet burbank for this recipe. You could use vintage cheddar or blue cheese instead of the smoked cheddar, if you like.

BASIC POTATO MASH

PREP + COOK TIME 30 MINUTES **SERVES** 4

1kg (2 pounds) potatoes (see tip), peeled, chopped coarsely •
40g (1½ ounces) butter • ¾ cup (180ml) hot milk

Place potatoes in a medium saucepan with enough cold water
to barely cover them. Boil, uncovered, over medium heat, for
15 minutes or until potato is tender; drain. Return potato to pan,
mash until smooth (or use a potato ricer or mouli). Add butter
and milk; fold in gently until mash is smooth. Season to taste.
Serve as is, or with one of the flavour variations, opposite.
tip Floury and all-rounder potatoes are best for mash; try
coliban, toolangi delight, king edward or dutch cream.

OLIVE OIL & SAGE MASH

Boil 1kg (2lbs) potatoes as directed for Basic Potato Mash (left); drain. Wipe pan dry. Heat ⅓ cup olive oil in same pan; fry 2 thinly sliced cloves garlic and 2 tablespoons sage leaves until crisp. Remove with a slotted spoon. Return potatoes to pan with ½ cup hot milk; mash until smooth. Season with salt and ground black pepper. Serve topped with garlic and sage.

LUXE MASH

Boil 1kg (2lbs) potatoes as directed for Basic Potato Mash (left); drain. Wipe pan dry. Mash potatoes in a heatproof bowl, or use a potato ricer, until smooth. Melt 60g (2oz) butter with ¾ cup mascarpone in same pan over medium heat; stir in mash and 30g (1oz) blue cheese. Season with salt and pepper. Serve topped with another 30g (1oz) crumbled blue cheese.

MUSTARD & CHEDDAR MASH

Make Basic Potato Mash (left). When adding the butter and milk, add 2 tablespoons dijon or wholegrain mustard and 1 cup coarsely grated vintage cheddar. Return pan to heat; stir mash over medium heat until smooth and cheddar melts. Season with salt and ground black pepper. Serve topped with extra grated vintage cheddar.

KALE MASH

Boil 1kg (2lbs) potatoes as directed for Basic Potato Mash (left); drain. Wipe pan dry. Heat ⅓ cup olive oil in pan; cook 125g (4oz) shredded kale and 1 chopped clove garlic, stirring, over medium heat for 5 minutes until kale wilts. Remove from pan. Return potatoes to pan with 30g (1oz) butter and ¾ cup hot milk; mash until smooth. Stir in kale; season with salt and pepper.

PERFECT ROAST POTATOES

PREP + COOK TIME 1 HOUR 10 MINUTES **SERVES** 4

6 pontiac potatoes (1.2kg), peeled, halved • ⅓ cup (80ml) olive oil • 50g
(1½ ounces) butter • 8 cloves garlic, unpeeled • ¼ cup fresh rosemary sprigs

Preheat oven to 220°C/425°F. Boil, steam or microwave potatoes for
5 minutes; drain. Pat dry with paper towel; cool 10 minutes. Gently rake
rounded side of potatoes with the tines of a fork. Place, cut-side down,
in a single layer, on an oiled oven tray. Brush with oil; dot with butter,
add garlic and rosemary. Roast 50 minutes, brushing occasionally with
oil mixture, or until potatoes are browned and crisp. Season with salt.
tip Dutch creams, coliban and sebago potatoes would also be suitable.

PREPARING THE POTATOES

Select similar sized potatoes; peel. Cut potatoes in half through the middle, then place in a saucepan of cold water. Bring to the boil; cook until just tender when pierced with a skewer. Drain well; pat dry with paper towel. Alternatively, microwave or steam.

RAKING PARCOOKED POTATOES

When potatoes are cool enough to handle, place cut-side down, on a chopping board. Rake the rounded side of each potato, using the tines of a fork. This allows the oil and butter to collect in the grooves, which makes the outside crisp.

THE ROASTING PAN

The pan you use will help with the crispness. Avoid ceramic; choose a heavy-based metal roasting pan that's not too deep. Oil the pan, then place potatoes, cut-side down, in a single layer. Brush potatoes with oil; dot with butter, then add garlic and rosemary.

ROASTING KIPFLER POTATOES

Preheat oven to 220°C/425°F. Cut 1.2kg (2½lbs) unpeeled kipfler (fingerling) potatoes in half lengthways. Place in a roasting pan with 2 halved bulbs garlic; season. Remove rind from 1 lemon in long thin strips. Drizzle with 2 tablespoons olive oil. Roast for 25 minutes or until golden and tender.

ROASTING CHAT POATOES

Preheat oven to 220°C/425°F. Cut 1.2kg (2½lbs) chat potatoes in half. Place in a roasting pan; sprinkle with 2 teaspoons fennel seeds and 1 teaspoon smoked paprika. Season with salt and freshly ground black pepper. Roast for 25 minutes, turning occasionally, or until golden and tender.

ROASTING KUMARA

Preheat oven to 220°C/425°F. Rinse 1.2kg (2½lbs) slender unpeeled kumara (orange sweet potatoes); pat dry with paper towel. Cut in half lengthways; place in a roasting pan with 8 cloves garlic and 8 sprigs thyme. Drizzle with 2 tablespoons olive oil; season. Roast 25 minutes until browned and tender.

WEDGES + FRIES

1. SPICY CAJUN POTATO WEDGES

Preheat oven to 220°C/425°F. Cut 1kg (2lbs) unpeeled kipfler (fingerling) potatoes into wedges. Combine 2 tablespoons olive oil, ½ teaspoon ground oregano, 2 teaspoons ground cumin, 1 teaspoon hot paprika, ½ teaspoon ground black pepper, 1 teaspoon ground coriander and ¼ teaspoon chilli powder in a small bowl. Place wedges on a large oiled oven tray, in a single layer; drizzle with oil mixture, toss to coat. Roast 40 minutes, turning ocassionally or until crisp and cooked. Serve topped with oregano leaves.

2. PAPRIKA POTATO WEDGES WITH PARMESAN

Place two baking trays in the oven; preheat oven to 240°C/475°F. Cut 1kg (2lbs) floury potatoes (sebago) into wedges. Place wedges in a large bowl with 2 tablespoons extra virgin olive oil, 40g (1½oz) melted butter and 2 teaspoons smoked paprika, then season with salt; toss to coat. Place wedges, in a single layer, on hot trays. Roast, turning once, for 35 minutes or until golden and crisp. Serve topped with ½ cup (40g) finely grated parmesan and with aïoli.

tip Aïoli is a garlic mayonnaise available from supermarkets and delis.

3. KUMARA WEDGES WITH LIME CHILLI SALT

Preheat oven to 240°C/475°F. Cut 1kg (2lbs) kumara (orange sweet potato) into wedges. Place wedges, in a single layer, on baking-paper-lined trays; drizzle wth 2 tablespoons olive oil. Roast 15 minutes. Turn wedges; roast a further 15 minutes or until lightly browned. Stir 2 teaspoons finely grated lime rind, 2 tablespoons sea salt flakes and 1 teaspoon chilli flakes in a small dry frying pan over a low heat for 3 minutes or until rind is dry. Cool. Serve wedges sprinkled with lime chilli salt.

4. LEMON PEPPER FRIES

Make a batch of fries following the Salted Fries (right) recipe, omitting the salt. Combine 1 tablespoon finely grated lemon rind (or use a microplane grater), ½ teaspoon freshly ground black pepper and 1 teaspoon salt flakes in a small bowl. Serve hot fries immediately sprinkled with lemon pepper and lemon wedges.

tips Use grated lime rind instead of lemon and crushed sichuan peppercorns instead of black pepper. These fries go well with battered or grilled fish or chicken, prawns and fish sandwiches.

5. SALTED FRIES

Cut 1kg (2lbs) peeled russet burbank potatoes, lengthways, into 1cm (½-inch) thick slices; cut lengthways into 1cm (½-inch) wide pieces. Place potato in a large bowl of cold water; stand for 30 minutes. Drain; pat dry with paper towel. Heat vegetable oil in a deep-fryer, large saucepan or wok; cook fries, in three batches, for 4 minutes each batch or until just tender but not browned (see General Techniques page 229). Drain fries on paper towel; stand 10 minutes. Reheat oil; cook fries again, in three batches, separating any that stick together, until crisp and golden. Drain on paper towel. Season with salt.

6. CHILLI GARLIC FRIES

Make a batch of fries following the Salted Fries (left) recipe. Meanwhile, heat 2 teaspoons olive oil in a small frying pan; cook 2 sliced fresh long red chillies until soft. Add 2 sliced cloves garlic; cook, stirring, until fragrant. Serve hot fries immediately sprinkled with chilli mixture.

tips If you like, add ½ cup thai basil leaves to the oil after cooking the fries; fry leaves for 30 seconds until crisp, then toss them with the chilli mixture. These fries go well with hamburgers, grilled or pan-fried steak and lamb cutlets.

1.

2.

3.

4.

5.

6.

ROASTED VEGETABLES

Match these good-looking vegetable dishes to any of the roast meats in our meat or chicken chapters,
or enjoy them as dishes in their own right, or as salads with the addition of a handful of salad leaves.

PARSNIP & PEAR
PREP + COOK TIME 40 MINUTES **SERVES** 4

Preheat oven to 200°C/400°F. Scrub and trim 4 medium (600g)
parsnips and core 2 medium (460g) pears. Cut parsnips and pears
lengthways into wedges. Line an oven tray with baking paper.
Place parsnips and pears on tray; drizzle with 2 tablespoons each
honey and extra virgin olive oil, then add 6 small sprigs fresh
rosemary. Season with salt and freshly ground black pepper; toss
to coat. Roast for 30 minutes or until parsnips and pears are
browned and tender. Add 2 slices torn prosciutto; roast a further
5 minutes or until crisp. Serve with roast chicken or turkey.

BEETROOT & WALNUT CRUMBLE
PREP + COOK TIME 1 HOUR **SERVES** 4

Preheat oven to 220°C/425°F. Trim leaves and stalks from 1.5kg
(3lbs) red beetroot (beets) and 500g (1lb) baby yellow beetroot
(beets); wash. Peel red beetroot; cut into six wedges. Keep yellow
ones whole. Place all beets on a large piece of foil on oven trays
with 2 bay leaves; drizzle with 1 tablespoon olive oil. Cover with
another piece of foil; seal. Roast red beets 40 minutes and yellow
beets 30 minute or until tender. Peel yellow beets; halve. Process
½ cup walnuts and ¼ cup fresh flat-leaf parsley until chopped.
Toss beetroots with walnut crumble. Serve with beef or lamb.

HEIRLOOM CARROTS
PREP + COOK TIME 40 MINUTES **SERVES** 6

Preheat oven to 200°C/400°F. Scrub 1 bunch each orange, white and purple heirloom carrots. Trim stalks to 2cm (¾-in) long; reserve carrot tops. You will need 1kg (2lbs) trimmed carrots. Pick 1 cup small tender leaves from reserved carrot tops, wash; discard remaining tops. Process tops with ½ cup extra virgin olive oil, ¼ cup red wine vinegar, 1 tablespoon honey and 2 teaspoons cumin seeds until finely chopped. Season to taste. Drizzle half the dressing over carrots; roast for 30 minutes or until tender. Serve topped with remaining dressing. Serve with pork or lamb.

KUMARA & CHICKPEAS
PREP + COOK TIME 45 MINUTES **SERVES** 4

Preheat oven to 220°C/425°F. Scrub 1kg (2lbs) small kumara (orange sweet potato). Cut kumara and 2 medium (340g) red onions lengthways into wedges. Drain 400g (12½oz) canned chickpeas (garbanzo beans); rinse. Place kumara, onions, chickpeas and 10 torn sprigs fresh thyme on a baking-paper-lined oven tray. Drizzle with ¼ cup olive oil; season with flaked salt and freshly ground black pepper; toss to coat. Roast for 30 minutes or until kumara is tender and browned. Serve with roast chicken, lamb or beef. For a vegetarian salad, toss with rocket.

KALE CAESAR SALAD

PREP + COOK TIME 40 MINUTES **SERVES** 4

½ loaf ciabatta (220g)

⅓ cup (80ml) olive oil

1 clove garlic, crushed

6 free-range egg, at room temperature

500g (1 pound) kale, trimmed, chopped coarsely

½ teaspoon sea salt

1 tablespoon olive oil, extra

½ cup (40g) shaved parmesan

buttermilk dressing

⅓ cup (80ml) buttermilk

2 tablespoons whole-egg mayonnaise

2 teaspoons lemon juice

1 teaspoon dijon mustard

1 anchovy fillet, chopped finely

½ clove garlic, crushed

1 Preheat oven to 180°C/350°F.

2 Tear bread into 2cm (¾-inch) pieces; place on a baking-paper-lined oven tray. Drizzle bread with oil, scatter with garlic; toss well to combine. Bake croûtons for 10 minutes or until golden.

3 Meanwhile, place eggs in a medium saucepan with enough cold water to cover; bring to the boil. Reduce heat; simmer, uncovered, for 4 minutes for soft boiled. Drain; refresh under cold running water. Peel eggs.

4 Make buttermilk dressing.

5 Place kale, salt and extra oil in a large bowl; rub well to soften the leaves (it will lose about half its volume). Add croûtons and half the dressing; toss gently to combine. Serve topped with halved eggs, parmesan and remaining dressing.

buttermilk dressing Place ingredients in a screw-top jar; shake well.

tip You could use baby kale leaves if you prefer, as they are softer and more tender than regular kale.

BASIC SALADS

GREEK SALAD

PREP TIME 15 MINUTES **SERVES** 4

4 ripe roma (egg) tomatoes (300g), cut into wedges •
2 lebanese cucumbers (260g), chopped coarsely • ¼ medium
red onion (45g), sliced thinly • ⅓ cup (60g) pitted kalamata
olives, halved • 150g (4½ ounces) fetta, crumbled coarsely •
½ teaspoon dried oregano leaves • ¼ cup (60ml) extra
virgin olive oil • 1 tablespoon red wine vinegar

Place tomato, cucumber, onion, olives and fetta in a large
bowl; toss gently to combine, sprinkle with oregano.
Place oil and vinegar in a screw-top jar; season, shake
well. Drizzle dressing over salad. Serve with fresh
oregano sprigs, if you like.

MIXED CABBAGE SLAW

PREP TIME 20 MINUTES **SERVES** 4

¼ cup (60ml) olive oil • 1 tablespoon white wine vinegar •
2 teaspoons wholegrain mustard • 1 tablespoon honey •
2 cups finely shredded green cabbage • 2 cups finely
shredded red cabbage • 2 cups finely shredded wombok
(napa cabbage) • 1 medium carrot (120g), grated coarsely •
4 green onions (scallions), sliced thinly

Whisk oil, vinegar, mustard and honey in a large bowl
then add remaining ingredients; toss gently to combine.
Salad is best served immediately.

TABBOULEH

PREP TIME 30 MINUTES (+ REFRIGERATION)

SERVES 4

¼ cup (50g) coarse burghul • ¼ cup boiling water •
3 medium tomatoes (450g) • 3 cups chopped fresh flat-leaf
parsley • 3 green onions (scallions), chopped finely • ¼ cup
coarsely chopped fresh mint • ¼ cup (60ml) lemon juice •
¼ cup (60ml) olive oil

Place burghul and the water in a small heatproof bowl.
Cover with plastic wrap; stand 10 minutes or until water
is absorbed. Seed and finely chop tomatoes (see Vegetable
Techniques page 198). Transfer burghul to a large bowl
with tomato and remaining ingredients; toss to combine.

HEIRLOOM TOMATO SALAD

PREP TIME 10 MINUTES

SERVES 4

900g (1¾lb) baby heirloom tomatoes, halved • 2 tablespoons
small fresh dill sprigs • 2 tablespoons small fresh basil
leaves • ¼ cup red-vein sorrel or baby spinach leaves •
150g (4½oz) soft marinated goat's cheese • 2 cloves garlic,
crushed • 2 tablespoons lemon juice • 1 tablespoon
olive oil • 2 teaspoons white vinegar

Place tomato and herbs in a medium bowl. Crumble
over goat's cheese. Place garlic, juice, oil and vinegar in
a screw-top jar; shake well. Drizzle dressing over salad;
toss gently to combine.

PEACH & ASPRAGUS CAPRESE SALAD

PREP + COOK TIME 25 MINUTES **SERVES** 4

340g (11 ounces) asparagus, trimmed

1½ tablespoons chilli oil

4 medium peaches (600g), halved, stones removed

4 medium heirloom tomatoes (600g), sliced if large, halved or quartered if small (see tips)

250g (8 ounces) buffalo mozzarella (see tips), torn

1 tablespoon white wine vinegar

½ cup fresh small basil leaves

pistachio mint pesto

½ cup (70g) pistachios

1½ cups fresh mint leaves

1 cup fresh flat-leaf parsley leaves

1 clove garlic, crushed

2 teaspoons finely grated lemon rind

2 teaspoons lemon juice

½ cup (125ml) extra virgin olive oil

1 Make pistachio mint pesto.

2 Place asparagus and 1 tablespoon of the chilli oil in a medium bowl; toss to coat. Season.

3 Cook asparagus, turning once, on a lightly oiled heated chargrill pan or barbecue flat plate for 10 minutes, adding the peaches to the pan for the last 2 minutes of asparagus cooking time, or until asparagus is tender and peaches are golden.

4 Layer peaches and tomatoes on a platter; top with asparagus and mozzarella, then drizzle with vinegar, remaining chilli oil and the pesto. Top with basil.

pistachio mint pesto Blend or process ingredients until smooth; season to taste.

tips Buffalo mozzarella has a tangier flavour than cow's milk mozzarella, which can be used instead. Slice larger varieties of heirloom tomatoes such as ox-hearts and cut medium or smaller types in half or into wedges.

CORN COBS + TOPPINGS

Cook 6 cobs corn (1.5kg), in husks in a large saucepan of boiling salted water for 6 minutes or until almost tender.
Drain; cool in husks. Peel back the corn husks; remove and discard the silks. Tie the husks back with kitchen string.
Heat a barbecue or chargrill pan over medium heat; cook corn, turning, for 5 minutes or until lightly charred.

DUKKAH SPRINKLE

Roast 2 teaspoons each cumin and coriander
seeds, ¼ cup each almonds, macadamias
and pistachios at 180°C/350°F, 8 minutes.
Cool. Process until chopped; add ¼ each
teaspoon salt, cinnamon and dried mint.
Brush cobs with olive oil; top with dukkah.

CORIANDER & LIME

Process 125g (4oz) chopped butter, 1 halved
clove garlic and 1 cup fresh coriander
(cilantro) until whipped and coriander
chopped. Add 2 teaspoons lime juice, season;
process to combine. Spread butter mixture
on cobs; sprinkle with fresh green chilli.

MEXICAN-STYLE MAYO

Process ¾ cup mayonnaise and 1 chilli in
adobe sauce (or ½ teaspoon smoked
paprika and ¼ teaspoon ground chilli)
until smooth. Spread mayonnaise mixture
on cobs; sprinkle with 1 cup finely grated
parmesan and a little smoked paprika.

AVOCADO & FETTA

Mash 2 small (400g) chopped ripe
avocados with 1 clove crushed garlic,
½ teaspoon each ground cumin and salt,
and 2 teaspoons lime juice in a small bowl.
Spread avocado mixture on cobs; top with
75g (2½oz) finely crumbled fetta.

TOMATO BACON CRUMBS

Cook 2 finely chopped bacon slices,
stirring, in a frying pan, for 5 minutes.
Stir in 1 tablespoon tomato paste, then
1 cup panko (japanese) breadcrumbs; cook,
stirring, 8 minutes until crisp. Spread ½ cup
mayonnaise on cobs; top with crumbs.

MISO BUTTER

Process 125g (4oz) chopped butter and
¼ cup white (shiro) miso until whipped.
Spread butter mixture on cobs; top with
1 finely chopped green onion (scallion)
and 2 tablespoons crushed wasabi-
flavoured dried peas.

CAESAR DRESSING

Place 1 egg in a small pan boiling water. Remove from heat, cover; stand 1 minute. Remove egg; cool. When cool enough to handle, break egg into a bowl; whisk in 2 crushed cloves garlic, ½ teaspoon dijon mustard and 2 finely chopped anchovy fillets. Gradually whisk in 1 cup olive oil in a thin stream, until thick and combined. Stir in 2 tablespoons lemon juice. Makes 1 cup.

TOMATO BASIL MAYONNAISE

Process 135g (4oz) coarsely chopped tomato, 1 cup mayonnaise and 2 tablespoons red wine vinegar in a food processor. Remove the seeds from 1 small fresh red chilli; finely chop. Add chopped chilli to mayonnaise mixture with 1 finely chopped green onion (scallion) and 1 tablespoon torn fresh basil leaves. Stir to combine. Makes 1½ cups.

BALSAMIC & GARLIC DRESSING

Whisk 2 tablespoons balsamic vinegar, ¼ cup lemon juice, 1 crushed clove garlic and ¾ cup olive oil in a small bowl until combined. Makes ½ cup.
Serve with robust salad leaves such as cos and raddichio.

CREAMY RANCH DRESSING

Blend ½ cup mayonnaise, ¼ cup buttermilk, 1 tablespoon white wine vinegar, 1 finely chopped small onion, 1 crushed clove garlic, 1 tablespoon each finely chopped fresh chives and fresh flat-leaf parsley, and ¼ teaspoon sweet paprika until combined. Makes 1½ cups.

CITRUS & POPPY SEED DRESSING

Whisk ⅔ cup (160g) sour cream, 2 teaspoons honey mustard,
1 teaspoon zested orange rind (see General Techniques page 228),
¼ cup orange juice, 2 tablespoons apple cider vinegar and 1 tablespoon
poppy seeds in a small bowl. Makes 1⅓ cups.
Goes with salmon, coleslaw and steamed green asparagus.

FRENCH DRESSING

Combine ⅓ cup white wine vinegar, 2 teaspoons dijon mustard and
½ teaspoon sugar in a small bowl. Gradually add ⅔ cup olive oil in a thin,
steady stream, whisking continuously until thickened. Makes 1⅓ cups.
Goes with most delicate and robust leafed salads, or an
heirloom tomato and basil salad. Add a little garlic if you like.

SESAME SOY DRESSING

Combine 1 tablespoon toasted sesame seeds, 1 tablespoon sesame oil,
2 finely chopped shallots, 2 tablespoons kecap manis and ¼ cup lime juice
in a small bowl. Makes ¾ cup. Goes well with blanched green vegetables,
prawns, steamed or pan-fried white fish and grilled chicken.

GREEN GODDESS DRESSING

Process the flesh of 1 small avocado, 1 cup mayonnaise, 2 finely chopped
anchovy fillets, 2 thinly sliced green onions, 2 teaspoons chopped fresh
flat-leaf parsley, chives and tarragon, and 2 teaspoons cider vinegar. Makes
1 cup. Serve with cos lettuce, steamed green vegetables and chicken salad.

BASIC STOCKS

BEEF

prep + cooking time 5 hours 10 minutes
(+ cooling & refrigeration) **makes** 3.5 litres (14 cups)

2kg (4 pounds) meaty beef bones

2 medium brown onions (300g), chopped coarsely

2 medium carrots (240g), chopped coarsely

2 stalks celery (300g), trimmed, chopped coarsely

5.5 litres (22 cups) water

3 bay leaves

2 teaspoons black peppercorns

3 litres (12 cups) water, extra

1 Preheat oven to 200°C/400°F.
2 Roast bones on an oven tray, uncovered, 1 hour or until browned.
3 Place bones in a large saucepan or stockpot with onion, carrot, celery, the water, bay leaves and peppercorns; bring to the boil. Reduce heat; simmer, uncovered, 3 hours, skimming surface occasionally. Add the extra water; simmer, uncovered, 1 hour.
4 Strain stock through a fine sieve into a large heatproof bowl; discard solids. Allow stock to cool. Cover; refrigerate until cold. Skim and discard surface fat before using.

CHICKEN

prep + cook time 2 hours 10 minutes
(+ cooling & refrigeration) **makes** 3.5 litres (14 cups)

2kg (4 pounds) chicken bones

2 medium onions (300g), chopped coarsely

2 medium carrots (240g), chopped coarsely

2 stalks celery (300g), trimmed, chopped coarsely

5 litres (20 cups) water

3 bay leaves

2 teaspoons black peppercorns

1 Place ingredients in a large saucepan or stockpot; simmer, uncovered, for 2 hours, skimming surface occasionally.
2 Strain stock through a fine sieve into a large heatproof bowl; discard solids. Allow stock to cool. Cover; refrigerate until cold. Skim and discard surface fat before using.

VEGETABLE

prep + cooking time 1 hour 40 minutes
(+ cooling & refrigeration) **makes** 3.5 litres (14 cups)

4 medium onions (600g), chopped coarsely

2 large carrots (360g), chopped coarsely

10 stalks celery (1.5kg), trimmed, chopped coarsely

2 large parsnips (700g), chopped coarsely

6 litres (24 cups) water

4 bay leaves

2 teaspoons black peppercorns

1 Place ingredients in a large saucepan; simmer,
uncovered, for 1½ hours.
2 Strain stock through a fine sieve into a large
heatproof bowl; discard solids. Allow stock to cool.
Cover; refrigerate until cold. Skim and discard any scum.

FISH

prep + cook time 25 minutes (+ cooling & refrigeration)
makes 2.5 litres (10 cups)

1.5kg (3 pounds) fish bones

3 litres (12 cups) water

1 medium onion (150g), chopped coarsely

2 stalks celery (300g), trimmed, chopped coarsely

2 bay leaves

1 teaspoon black peppercorns

1 Place ingredients in a large saucepan; simmer,
uncovered, for 20 minutes.
2 Strain stock through a fine sieve into a large
heatproof bowl; discard solids. Allow stock to cool.
Cover; refrigerate until cold. Skim and discard surface
fat before using.

Cool stock as rapidly as possible, before being refrigerated by placing the saucepan in a sink of iced water, reaching halfway up the side of the pan. Stir frequently to release the heat. All stocks will keep in an airtight container in the fridge for up to 3 days or freeze for up to 3 months. Bring stock to the boil before using.

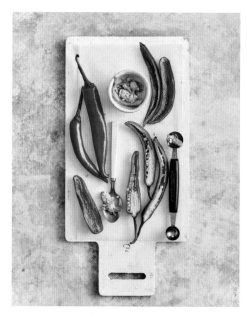

HOW TO CHOP AN ONION

Peel onion, leaving the root end intact. Cut in half lengthways; place flat-side down. Cut parallel vertical slices, starting just after the root end. Holding onion on top with one hand, hold the knife horizontally in the other and cut twice. Finally, cut thin slices widthways, opposite to the first cuts.

GREEN ONION (SCALLION) CURLS

Trim root end and tops of onions slightly; cut into 8cm (3¾-inch) lengths. Cut each length in half lengthways, then slice lengthways again into thin strips. Alternatively, use a green onion shredder tool. Buy online or from Asian grocers. Place strips in a bowl of iced water for 10 minutes to curl.

SEEDING FRESH CHILLIES

Cut chillies in half lengthways, then run a spoon or melon baller down the length of the chilli to scoop up the seeds; discard seeds. Make sure not to touch your eyes when handling chillies and to wash your hands after handling them. If you have cuts on your hands or sensitive skin wear disposable gloves.

TOOLS FOR SLICING

For vegetable ribbons use a mandoline or V-slicer, making sure to always use the hand guard. You can also use a vegetable peeler for narrow vegetables. To cut vegetables into julienne (matchsticks), use the julienne cutting blade on the slicer or a vegetable stripper or julienne peeler, from Asian grocers.

ZESTING CITRUS RIND

To cut lemon (lime or orange) rind into strips, run a zesting tool from top to bottom over the fruit. The strips can be used immediately. To curl and crisp the strips, place them in a bowl of iced water for 5-10 minutes. Use the strips or curls as both a garnish and flavouring.

SEGMENTING ORANGES

Cut top and bottom from an orange with a small sharp knife. Cut remaining rind and white pith from orange, following the curve of the fruit. Holding orange over a bowl, cut down both sides of the white membrane to release each segment. Squeeze juice from membrane in bowl.

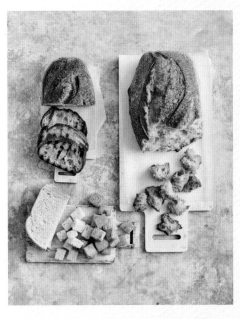

STORING HERBS

Treat basil like a bunch of flowers and store upright in water, covered with a plastic bag, rather than the fridge. Other soft and hard herbs are best wrapped in dampened paper towel and placed into airtight containers or bags. To revive soft-leaf herbs place in a bowl of iced water. Mico herbs require snipping.

MAKING BREADCRUMBS

Breadcrumbs are best made from bread that's at least a day-old, if it is too moist it won't process well. Remove bread crust, then cut into small pieces. Process, in batches, using the pulse button, until crumbs form. Use immediately or package into zip-top plastic bags and freeze for up to 3 months.

CROUTONS & GRILLED BREAD

To make croûtons from sliced white bread, cut it into cubes. For rustic-style bread, tear the bread. Cook cubes in a little hot oil, turning until golden. Roast torn bread, drizzled with olive oil, 15 minutes. For chargrill bread, brush slices with olive oil; cook a few minutes each side on a heated chargrill pan.

MARINATING

A zip-top plastic bag is a great way to marinate or coat foods with a spice rubs. Place the food and the marinade, or spice rub into the bag; remove air and seal the top tightly. Massage the food through the bag to coat. Place the bag on its side on a tray; refrigerate, turning occasionally.

STIR FRYING

The trick to successful stir-frying is to have everything ready and cut into even pieces. The temperature is also very important, it needs to be high and the cooking brief. It helps to heat the wok first before adding the oil. Add ingredients as per the recipe, taking care not to overcrowd the wok.

DEEP FRYING

Ensure that the pan you are using is dry, before filling it one-third full with oil. The general temperature for frying is 180°C/350°F, unless instructed otherwise. Use a cooking thermometer to gauge the temperature, or drop a cube of bread into to the oil; it should sizzle rapidly and start to brown.

GLOSSARY

ALLSPICE also known as pimento or jamaican pepper; so-named because it tastes like a combination of nutmeg, cumin, clove and cinnamon. Available whole or ground.

ALMONDS flat, pointy-tipped nuts with a pitted brown shell that encloses a creamy white kernel covered by a brown skin.

blanched brown skins removed from the kernel.

flaked paper-thin slices of blanched or natural almonds.

ground also called almond meal; almonds are powdered to a coarse flour-like texture.

natural almond kernels with the brown skin on.

slivered small pieces cut lengthways.

ANCHOVIES small oily fish. Anchovy fillets are preserved and packed in oil or salt in small cans or jars, and are strong in flavour. Fresh anchovies are much milder in flavour.

ARTICHOKE, GLOBE large flower-bud member of the thistle family; it has tough petal-like leaves, and is edible in part when cooked. The tender centre (heart) can be harvested from the plant after the prickly choke is removed. Cooked hearts can be bought from delicatessens or canned in brine.

BACON also known as bacon slices or rashers.

BAKING PAPER also called parchment or baking parchment; a silicone-coated paper that is primarily used for lining baking pans and oven trays so cooked food doesn't stick, making removal easy.

BAKING POWDER a raising agent consisting mainly of two parts cream of tartar to one part bicarbonate of soda (baking soda).

BARLEY a nutritious grain used in soups and stews. Hulled barley, the least processed, is high in fibre. Pearl barley has had the husk removed then steamed and polished so that only the "pearl" of the original grain remains, much the same as white rice.

BAY LEAVES aromatic leaves from the bay tree available fresh or dried; adds a strong, slightly peppery flavour.

BEANS

broad (fava) available dried, fresh, canned and frozen. Fresh should be peeled twice (discarding the outer long green pod and the beige-green tough inner shell); frozen beans have had their pods removed but the beige shell still needs removal.

butter cans labelled butter beans are, in fact, cannellini beans. Confusingly butter is also another name for lima beans (dried and canned); a large beige bean having a mealy texture and mild taste.

cannellini a small white bean similar in appearance and flavour to other white beans (great northern, navy or haricot), all of which can be substituted for the other. Available dried or canned.

kidney medium-sized red bean, slightly floury in texture, yet sweet in flavour.

snake long (about 40cm/16 inches), thin, round, fresh green bean; Asian in origin with a taste similar to green beans. Are also known as yard-long beans because of their (pre-metric) length.

white a generic term we use for canned cannellini, haricot, navy or great northern beans of the same family; all can be used.

BEEF

blade from the shoulder; isn't as tender as other cuts, so it needs slow-roasting.

chuck from the neck and shoulder of the beef; tends to be chewy but flavourful and inexpensive. A good cut for stewing or braising.

eye-fillet also known as beef tenderloin; fine textured, extremely tender and more expensive than other cuts.

gravy beef boneless stewing beef from shin; slow-cooked, imbues stocks, soups and casseroles with a gelatine richness. Cut crossways, with bone in, is osso buco.

minced also known as ground beef.

osso buco literally meaning 'bone with a hole', osso buco is cut from the shin of the hind leg. It is also known as knuckle.

rump boneless tender cut taken from the upper part of the round (hindquarter). Cut into steaks, good for barbecuing; as one piece, great as a roast.

scotch fillet cut from the muscle running behind the shoulder along the spine. Also known as cube roll, cuts include standing rib roast and rib-eye.

short ribs cut from the rib section; usually larger, more tender and meatier than pork spare ribs.

skirt steak lean, flavourful coarse-grained cut from the inner thigh. Needs slow-cooking; good for stews or casseroles.

BEETROOT (BEETS) firm, round root vegetable.

BICARBONATE OF SODA (BAKING SODA) a raising agent.

BREAD

ciabatta in Italian, the word means slipper, the traditional shape of this popular crisp-crusted, open-textured white sourdough bread.

pitta also known as lebanese bread. This wheat-flour pocket bread is sold in large, flat pieces that separate into two thin rounds. Also available in small thick pieces called pocket pitta.

sourdough so-named, not because it's sour in taste, but because it's made by using a small amount of 'starter dough', which contains a yeast culture, mixed into flour and water. Part of the resulting dough is then saved to use as the starter dough next time.

tortilla thin, round unleavened bread; can be made at home or purchased frozen, fresh or vacuum-packed. Two kinds are available, one made from wheat flour and the other from corn.

turkish also called pide. Sold in long flat loaves and individual rounds; made from wheat flour and sprinkled with black onion seeds.

BREADCRUMBS

fresh bread, usually white, processed into crumbs.

packaged prepared fine-textured but crunchy white breadcrumbs; good for coating foods that are to be fried.

panko (japanese) are available in two kinds: larger pieces and fine crumbs; have a lighter texture than Western-style ones. Available from Asian food stores and most supermarkets.

stale crumbs made by grating, blending or processing 1- or 2-day-old bread. See also General Techniques page 229.

BROCCOLINI a cross between broccoli and chinese kale; it has long asparagus-like stems with a long loose floret, both are edible. Resembles broccoli but is milder and sweeter in taste.

BURGHUL also called bulgar wheat; hulled steamed wheat kernels that, once dried, are crushed into various sized grains. Used in Middle Eastern dishes such as felafel, kibbeh and tabbouleh. Is not the same as cracked wheat.

BUTTER use salted or unsalted (sweet) butter; 125g (4 ounces) is equal to one stick of butter.

CAPERS grey-green buds of a warm climate shrub (usually Mediterranean); sold dried and salted or pickled in a vinegar brine. Rinse before using.

CAPSICUM (BELL PEPPER) comes in many colours: red, green, yellow and orange. Discard seeds and membranes before use.

CARDAMOM a spice native to India and used extensively in its cuisine; can be purchased in pod, seed or ground form. Has a distinctive aromatic, sweetly rich flavour.

CAVOLO NERO (TUSCAN CABBAGE) it has long, narrow, wrinkled leaves and a rich and astringent, mild cabbage flavour. It doesn't lose its volume like silver beet or spinach when cooked, but it does need longer cooking.

CELERIAC (CELERY ROOT) tuberous root with knobbly brown skin, white flesh and a celery-like flavour. Keep peeled celeriac in acidulated water to stop it discolouring. It can be grated and eaten raw in salads; used in stews; mashed like potatoes; or sliced and deep-fried as chips.

CHEESE

fetta Greek in origin; a crumbly textured goat- or sheep-milk cheese with a sharp, salty taste. Ripened and stored in salted whey.

fetta, persian a soft, creamy fetta marinated in a blend of olive oil, garlic, herbs and spices; available from most major supermarkets.

goat's made from goat's milk, has an earthy, strong taste; available in both soft and firm textures, in various shapes and sizes, and sometimes rolled in ash or herbs.

gruyère a hard-rind Swiss cheese with small holes and a nutty, slightly salty flavour. A popular cheese for soufflés.

haloumi a firm, cream-coloured sheep-milk cheese matured in brine; haloumi can be grilled or fried, briefly, without breaking down. Should be eaten while still warm as it becomes tough and rubbery on cooling.

mozzarella soft, spun-curd cheese; originating in southern Italy where it was traditionally made from water-buffalo milk. Now generally made from cow's milk, it is the most popular pizza cheese because of its low melting point and elasticity when heated.

parmesan also called parmigiano; is a hard, grainy cow-milk cheese originating in Italy. Reggiano is the best variety.

pecorino the Italian generic name for cheeses made from sheep milk; hard, white to pale-yellow in colour. If you can't find it, use parmesan instead.

ricotta a soft, sweet, moist, white cow-milk cheese with a low fat content and a slightly grainy texture. The name roughly translates as 'cooked again' and refers to ricotta's manufacture from a whey that is itself a by-product of other cheese making.

CHICKEN

barbecued when cooked chicken is called for in our recipes, we use whole barbecued chickens weighing about 900g (1¾ pounds) each. Skin discarded and bones removed, this size chicken provides 4 cups (400g) shredded meat or about 3 cups (400g) coarsely chopped meat.

breast fillet breast halved, skinned and boned.

drumsticks leg with skin and bone intact.

maryland leg and thigh still connected in a single piece; bones and skin intact.

small chicken also known as spatchcock or poussin; no more than 6 weeks old, weighing a maximum of 500g (1 pound). Also a cooking term to describe splitting a small chicken open, flattening out then grilling.

thigh skin and bone intact.

thigh cutlets thigh with skin and centre bone intact; sometimes found skinned with bone intact.

thigh fillets the skin and bone removed.

CHICKPEAS (GARBANZO BEANS) an irregularly round, sandy-coloured legume. Has a firm texture even after cooking, a floury mouth-feel and robust nutty flavour; available canned or dried (soak for several hours in cold water before use).

CHILLI available in many types and sizes. Use rubber gloves when seeding and chopping fresh chillies as they can burn your skin. Removing membranes and seeds lessens the heat level.

flakes dried, deep-red, dehydrated chilli slices and whole seeds.

green any unripened chilli; also some particular varieties that are ripe when green, such as jalapeño, habanero, poblano or serrano.

jalapeño pronounced hah-lah-pain-yo. Fairly hot, medium-sized, plump, dark green chilli; available pickled, sold canned or bottled, and fresh, from greengrocers.

long red available both fresh and dried; a generic term used for any moderately hot, thin, long (6-8cm/2¼-3¼ inch) chilli.

powder can be used as a substitute for fresh chillies (½ teaspoon ground chilli powder to 1 chopped medium fresh chilli).

thai (serrano) also known as "scuds"; tiny, very hot and bright red in colour.

CHINESE COOKING WINE (SHAO HSING) also called chinese rice wine; made from fermented rice, wheat, sugar and salt. Found in Asian food shops; if you can't find it, use mirin or sherry.

CHINESE FIVE SPICE POWDER a fragrant mixture of ground cinnamon, cloves, star anise, sichuan pepper and fennel seeds. Used in Chinese and other Asian cooking; available from most supermarkets or Asian food shops.

CHORIZO SAUSAGES a sausage of Spanish origin, made from coarsely minced (ground) smoked pork and highly seasoned with garlic, chilli powder and other spices.

CHOY SUM a member of the buk choy family; easy to identify with its long stems, light green leaves and yellow flowers. Stems and leaves are both edible, steamed or stir-fried.

COCONUT

cream obtained from the first pressing of the coconut flesh alone, without the addition of water; the second pressing (less rich) is sold as coconut milk. Available in cans and cartons from supermarkets.

flaked dried flaked coconut flesh.

milk not the liquid inside the fruit (coconut water), but the diluted liquid from the second pressing of the white flesh of a mature coconut. Available in cans and cartons at most supermarkets.

shredded thin strips of dried coconut.

CORIANDER (CILANTRO) also known as pak chee or chinese parsley; a bright-green leafy herb with a pungent flavour. Both stems and roots of coriander are also used in cooking; wash well before using. Also available ground or as seeds; these should not be substituted for fresh as the tastes are completely different.

CORNFLOUR (CORNSTARCH) available made from corn or wheat (wheaten cornflour, gluten-free, gives a lighter texture in cakes); used as a thickening agent in cooking.

COS (ROMAINE) LETTUCE the traditional caesar salad lettuce. Long, with leaves ranging from dark green on the outside to almost white near the core; the leaves have a stiff centre rib giving a slight cupping effect to the leaf on either side.

COUSCOUS a fine, dehydrated, grain-like cereal product made from semolina; it swells to three or four times its original size when liquid is added. It is eaten like rice with a tagine, as a side dish or salad ingredient.

CRANBERRIES available dried and frozen; has a rich, astringent flavour and can be used in sweet and savoury dishes. The dried version can usually be substituted for or with other dried fruit.

CREAM

pouring also called pure or fresh cream. It has no additives and contains a minimum fat content of 35%.

thick (double) dolloping cream with a minimum fat content of 45%.

thickened (heavy) a whipping cream that contains a thickener. It has a minimum fat content of 35%.

CUMIN also known as zeera or comino; has a spicy, nutty flavour.

CURRY PASTES some recipes in this book call for commercially prepared pastes of varying strengths and flavours. Use whichever one you feel best suits your spice-level tolerance.

DAIKON this long, white horseradish has a wonderful, sweet flavour. After peeling, eat it raw in salads or shredded; sliced or cubed and cooked in stir-fries and casseroles. The flesh is white but the skin can be either white or black; buy those that are firm and unwrinkled from Asian food shops.

DUKKAH an Egyptian specialty spice mixture made up of roasted nuts, seeds and an array of aromatic spices.

EGGPLANT also called aubergine. Ranging in size from tiny to very large and in colour from pale green to deep purple. Can also be purchased char-grilled, packed in oil, in jars.

EGGWASH beaten egg (white, yolk or both) and milk or water; often brushed over pastry or bread to impart colour or gloss.

FENNEL a white to very pale green-white, firm, crisp, roundish vegetable about 8-12cm (3¼-4¾ inches) in diameter. The bulb has a slightly sweet, anise flavour but the leaves have a much stronger taste. Also the name of dried seeds having a licorice flavour.

FISH SAUCE called nam pla (Thai) or nuoc nam (Vietnamese); made from pulverised salted fermented fish, most often anchovies. Has a pungent smell and strong taste, so use sparingly.

FLOUR

plain (all-purpose) a general all-purpose wheat flour.

self-raising plain flour sifted with baking powder in the proportion of 1 cup flour to 2 teaspoons baking powder.

GAI LAN also known as chinese broccoli, gai larn, kanah, gai lum and chinese kale; used more for its stems than its coarse leaves.

GARAM MASALA a blend of spices that includes cardamom, cinnamon, coriander, cloves, fennel and cumin. Black pepper and chilli can be added for heat.

GHEE also called clarified butter; with the milk solids removed, this fat has a high smoking point so can be heated to a high temperature without burning. Commonly used in Indian cooking.

GINGER

fresh also called green or root ginger; the thick gnarled root of a tropical plant.

ground also called powdered ginger; used as a flavouring in baking but cannot be substituted for fresh ginger.

GREASING/OILING PANS use butter (for sweet baking), oil or cooking-oil spray (for savoury baking) to grease baking pans; overgreasing pans can cause food to overbrown. Use paper towel or a pastry brush to spread the oil or butter over the pan.

HARISSA a Moroccan paste made from dried chillies, cumin, garlic, oil and caraway seeds. Available from Middle Eastern food shops and supermarkets.

HOISIN SAUCE a thick, sweet and spicy Chinese paste made from salted fermented soya beans, onions and garlic.

ICEBERG LETTUCE a heavy, firm round lettuce with tightly packed leaves and crisp texture.

KAFFIR LIME also called magrood. The wrinkled, bumpy-skinned green fruit of a small citrus tree. As a rule, only the rind and leaves are used.

KAFFIR LIME LEAVES also called bai magrood. Aromatic leaves of a citrus tree; two glossy dark green leaves joined end to end, forming a rounded hourglass shape. A strip of fresh lime peel may be substituted for each kaffir lime leaf.

KECAP MANIS a thick soy sauce with added sugar and spices. The sweetness comes from the addition of molasses or palm sugar.

KITCHEN STRING made of a natural product such as cotton or hemp so that it neither affects the flavour of the food it's tied around nor melts when heated.

KUMARA (ORANGE SWEET POTATO) the Polynesian name of an orange-fleshed sweet potato often confused with yam.

LAMB

backstrap also called eye of loin; the larger fillet from a row of loin chops or cutlets. Tender, best cooked rapidly: barbecued or pan-fried.

cutlet small, tender rib chop; sometimes sold french-trimmed, with all the fat and gristle at the narrow end of the bone removed.

fillets fine texture, most expensive and extremely tender.

leg cut from the hindquarter; can be boned, butterflied, rolled and tied, or cut into dice.

rolled shoulder boneless section of the forequarter, rolled and secured with string or netting.

shank forequarter leg; sometimes sold as drumsticks or frenched shanks if the gristle and narrow end of the bone are discarded and the remaining meat trimmed.

shoulder large, tasty piece having much connective tissue so is best pot-roasted or braised. Makes the best mince.

LEMON GRASS a tall, clumping, lemon-smelling and -tasting, sharp-edged grass; the white part of the stem is used, chopped, in cooking.

LENTILS (red, brown, yellow) dried pulses often identified by and named after their colour. Eaten by cultures all over the world, most famously in the dhals of India, lentils have high food value.

French-style green lentils related to the famous french lentils du puy; these green-blue, tiny lentils have a nutty, earthy flavour and a hardy nature that allows them to be rapidly cooked without disintegrating. Are also called australian, bondi or matilda lentils.

MAPLE SYRUP, PURE distilled from the sap of sugar maple trees found only in Canada and the USA. Maple-flavoured syrup or pancake syrup is not an adequate substitute for the real thing.

MIRIN a Japanese champagne-coloured cooking wine, made of glutinous rice and alcohol. It is used just for cooking.

MIXED SPICE a classic spice mixture generally containing caraway, allspice, coriander, cumin, nutmeg and ginger, although cinnamon and other spices can be added.

MOROCCAN SEASONING available from most Middle-Eastern food stores, spice shops and major supermarkets. A ground blend of turmeric, cinnamon and cumin.

MORTAR AND PESTLE a cooking tool whose design has remained the same over the centuries: the mortar is a bowl-shaped container and the pestle a rounded, bat-shaped tool. Together, they grind and pulverise spices, herbs and other foods. The pestle is pressed against the mortar and rotated, grinding the ingredient between the two surfaces. Essential for curry pastes and crushing spices.

MUSHROOMS

button small, cultivated white mushrooms with a mild flavour.

dried porcini also known as cèpes; the richest-flavoured mushrooms. Expensive, but because they're so strongly flavoured, only a small amount is required.

enoki cultivated mushrooms; tiny long-stemmed, pale mushrooms that grow and are sold in clusters, and can be used that way or separated by slicing off the base. They have a mild fruity flavour and are slightly crisp in texture.

flat large, flat mushrooms with a rich earthy flavour, ideal for filling and barbecuing. They are sometimes misnamed field mushrooms which are wild mushrooms.

portobello are mature, fully opened swiss browns; they are larger and bigger in flavour.

shiitake, fresh also known as chinese black, forest or golden oak mushrooms; although cultivated, they are large and meaty and have the earthiness and taste of wild mushrooms.

swiss brown also known as cremini or roman mushrooms; are light brown mushrooms with a full-bodied flavour.

MUSTARD

dijon pale brown, distinctively flavoured, mild french mustard.

wholegrain also called seeded mustard. A french-style coarse-grain mustard made from crushed mustard seeds and dijon-style french mustard.

NUTMEG a strong and pungent spice ground from the dried nut of an evergreen tree native to Indonesia. Usually found ground but the flavour is more intense from a whole nut, available from spice shops, so it's best to grate your own.

OIL

cooking spray we use a cooking spray made from canola oil.

olive made from ripened olives. Extra virgin and virgin are the first and second press, respectively, of the olives; "extra light" or "light" on other types refers to taste not fat levels.

peanut pressed from ground peanuts; most commonly used oil in Asian cooking because of its capacity to handle high heat without burning (high smoke point).

sesame used as a flavouring rather than a cooking medium.

ONIONS

brown and white are interchangeable; white onions have a more pungent flesh.

green (scallions) also called, incorrectly, shallot; an immature onion picked before the bulb has formed, has a long, bright-green stalk.

red also known as spanish, red spanish or bermuda onion; a sweet-flavoured, large, purple-red onion.

shallots also called french or golden shallots or eschalots; small and brown-skinned.

spring an onion with a small white bulb and long, narrow green-leafed tops.

PANCETTA an Italian unsmoked bacon; pork belly cured in salt and spices then rolled into a sausage shape and dried for several weeks. Used as an ingredient rather than eaten on its own.

PAPRIKA ground, dried, sweet red capsicum (bell pepper); available as sweet, hot, mild and smoked.

PARSLEY a versatile herb with a fresh, earthy flavour. There are about 30 varieties of curly parsley; the flat-leaf variety (also called continental or italian parsley) is stronger in flavour and darker in colour.

PARSNIP their nutty sweetness is especially good when steamed and dressed with a garlic and cream sauce or in a curried parsnip soup, or simply baked. Can be substituted for potatoes. Available all year but the cold develops their sweet/savoury flavour in winter.

PASTRY SHEETS ready-rolled packaged sheets of frozen puff and shortcrust pastry, available from supermarkets.

PEPITAS (PUMPKIN SEEDS) are the pale green kernels of dried pumpkin seeds; they can be bought plain or salted.

PINE NUTS not a nut but a small, cream-coloured kernel from pine cones. Toast before use to bring out their flavour.

POLENTA also known as cornmeal; a flour-like cereal made of ground corn (maize). Also the name of the dish made from it.

POMEGRANATE dark-red, leathery-skinned fruit about the size of an orange filled with hundreds of seeds, each wrapped in an edible lucent-crimson pulp with a unique tangy sweet-sour flavour.

POMEGRANATE MOLASSES not to be confused with pomegranate syrup or grenadine (used in cocktails); pomegranate molasses is thicker, browner, and more concentrated in flavour — tart and sharp, slightly sweet and fruity. Brush over grilling or roasting meat, seafood or poultry, add to salad dressings or sauces. Buy from Middle Eastern food stores or specialty food shops.

PORK

belly fatty cut sold in rashers or a piece, with or without rind or bone.

cutlets cut from ribs.

loin chops or roasting cut from the loin.

neck sometimes called pork scotch; a boneless cut from the foreloin.

shoulder joint sold with the bone in or out.

spare ribs (american-style spareribs); well-trimmed mid-loin ribs.

POTATOES

coliban round, smooth white skin and flesh; good for baking and mashing.

desiree oval, smooth and pink-skinned, waxy yellow flesh; good in salads, boiled and roasted.

idaho also called russet burbank; russet in colour, fabulous baked.

king edward slightly plump and rosy; great mashed.

kipfler (kipfler) small, finger-shaped, nutty flavour; great baked and in salads.

lasoda round, red skin with deep eyes, white flesh; good for mashing or roasting.

pontiac large, red skin, deep eyes, white flesh; good grated, boiled and baked.

ruby lou oval, with dark pink skin and shallow eyes; has a white flesh and is good for roasting and salads.

russet burbank long and oval, rough white skin with shallow eyes, white flesh; good for baking and frying.

sebago white skin, oval; good fried, mashed and baked.

spunta large, long, yellow flesh, floury; great mashed and fried.

PRESERVED LEMON RIND a North African specialty; lemons are quartered and preserved in salt and lemon juice or water. To use, remove and discard pulp, squeeze juice from rind, rinse rind well; slice thinly. Once opened, store under refrigeration.

PROSCIUTTO a kind of unsmoked Italian ham; salted, air-cured and aged, it is usually eaten uncooked.

QUINOA pronounced keen-wa; is a gluten-free grain. It has a delicate, slightly nutty taste and chewy texture. Available red, white and tri-coloured.

RADICCHIO Italian in origin; a member of the chicory family. The dark burgundy leaves and strong, bitter flavour can be cooked or eaten raw in salads. Comes in varieties named after their places of origin, such as round-headed Verona or long-headed Treviso.

RAS EL HANOUT a classic spice blend used in Moroccan cooking. The name means 'top of the shop' and is the very best spice blend a spice merchant has to offer. Most versions contain over a dozen spices, including cardamom, nutmeg, mace, cinnamon and ground chilli.

RICE

arborio small, round grain rice well-suited to absorb a large amount of liquid; the high level of starch makes it especially suitable for risottos for its classic creaminess.

basmati a white, fragrant long-grained rice; the grains fluff up when cooked. Wash grains several times before cooking.

brown retains the high-fibre, nutritious bran coating that's removed from white rice when hulled. It takes longer to cook than white rice and has a chewier texture. Once cooked, the long grains stay separate, while the short grains are soft and stickier.

jasmine is a long-grain white rice recognised around the world as having a perfumed aromatic quality; moist in texture, it clings together after cooking. Sometimes substituted for basmati rice.

ROASTING/TOASTING desiccated coconut, pine nuts and sesame seeds roast more evenly if stirred over low heat in a heavy-based frying pan; their natural oils will help turn them golden. Remove from pan immediately. Nuts and dried coconut can be roasted in the oven to release their aromatic essential oils. Spread evenly onto an oven tray, roast at 180°C/350°F for about 5 minutes.

ROCKET (ARUGULA) also called rugula and rucola; peppery green leaf eaten raw in salads or used in cooking. Baby rocket leaves are smaller and less peppery.

SAGE pungent herb with narrow, grey-green leaves; slightly bitter with a slightly musty mint aroma. Refrigerate fresh sage wrapped in a paper towel and sealed in a plastic bag for up to 4 days.

SAFFRON available ground or in strands; imparts a yellow-orange colour to food once infused. The quality can vary greatly; the best is the most expensive spice in the world.

SEAFOOD

fish fillets, firm white blue eye, bream, flathead, snapper, ling, swordfish, whiting, jewfish or sea perch are all good choices. Check for small pieces of bone and use tweezers to remove them.

marinara mix a mixture of uncooked, chopped seafood available from fishmarkets and fishmongers.

mussels must be tightly closed when bought, indicating they are alive. Before cooking, scrub the shells with a strong brush and remove the 'beards' (see also Seafood Techniques page 111). Some mussels might not open – you do not have to discard these, just open with a knife and cook a little more if you wish. Varieties include black and green-lip.

ocean trout a farmed fish with pink, soft flesh. From the same family as the atlantic salmon; one can be substituted for the other.

octopus usually tenderised before you buy them; both octopus and squid require either long slow cooking (for large molluscs) or quick cooking over high heat (for small molluscs) – anything in between will make the octopus tough and rubbery.

prawns (shrimp) varieties include, school, king, royal red, sydney harbour, tiger. Can be bought uncooked (green) or cooked, with or without shells.

salmon red-pink firm flesh with few bones; moist delicate flavour.

SILVER BEET (SWISS CARD) also called, incorrectly, spinach; has fleshy stalks and large leaves. Prepare as you would spinach.

SOY SAUCE made from fermented soya beans. Several variations are available in most supermarkets and Asian food stores. We use japanese soy sauce unless stated otherwise.

SPINACH also called english spinach and incorrectly, silver beet. Baby spinach leaves are eaten raw in salads or cooked until wilted.

STAR ANISE dried star-shaped pod with an astringent aniseed flavour; used to flavour stocks and marinades. Available whole and ground, it is an essential ingredient in chinese five spice.

SUGAR

brown very soft, finely granulated sugar retaining molasses for its characteristic colour and flavour.

caster (superfine) finely granulated table sugar.

icing (confectioners') also called powdered sugar; pulverised granulated sugar crushed with a little cornflour (cornstarch).

palm also called nam tan pip, jaggery, jawa or gula melaka; made from the sap of the sugar palm tree. Light brown to black in colour and usually sold in rock-hard cakes; use brown sugar instead.

pure icing (confectioners') also known as powdered sugar.

raw natural brown granulated sugar.

white (granulated) coarse, granulated table sugar, also called crystal sugar.

SUMAC a purple-red, astringent spice ground from berries growing on shrubs flourishing wild around the Mediterranean; adds a tart, lemony flavour to food. Available from supermarkets.

TAMARI a thick, dark soy sauce made mainly from soya beans, but without the wheat used in most standard soy sauces.

TAMARIND the tamarind tree produces clusters of hairy brown pods, each of which is filled with seeds and a viscous pulp, that are dried and pressed into the blocks of tamarind found in Asian food shops. Gives a sweet-sour, slightly astringent taste to marinades, pastes, sauces and dressings.

TAMARIND CONCENTRATE (OR PASTE) the distillation of tamarind pulp into a condensed, compacted paste. Thick and purple-black, it requires no soaking. Found in Asian food stores.

TOFU also called bean curd; an off-white, custard-like product made from the "milk" of crushed soybeans. Comes fresh as soft or firm, and processed as fried or pressed dried sheets. Fresh tofu can be refrigerated in water (changed daily) for up to 4 days.

TOMATOES

bottled pasta sauce a prepared sauce; a blend of tomatoes, herbs and spices.

canned whole peeled tomatoes in natural juices; available crushed, chopped or diced. Use undrained.

passata sieved tomato puree; contains no flavourings. Available from supermarkets alongside bottled pasta sauce.

paste triple-concentrated tomato puree used to flavour soups, stews and sauces.

roma (egg) also called plum; these are smallish, oval-shaped tomatoes much used in Italian cooking or salads.

truss small vine-ripened tomatoes with vine still attached.

WATERCRESS one of the cress family, a large group of peppery greens. Highly perishable, so must be used as soon as possible after purchase. It has an exceptionally high vitamin K content, which is great for eye health, and is an excellent source of calcium.

WOMBOK (NAPA CABBAGE) also called chinese cabbage; elongated in shape with pale green, crinkly leaves, is the most common cabbage in South-East Asia. Can be shredded or chopped and eaten raw or braised, steamed or stir-fried.

WORCESTERSHIRE SAUCE thin, dark-brown spicy sauce developed by the British when in India; used as a seasoning for meat, gravies and cocktails, and as a condiment.

YOGHURT we use plain full-cream yoghurt unless stated.

greek-style plain yoghurt strained in a cloth (muslin) to remove the whey and to give it a creamy consistency.

ZUCCHINI also called courgette; small, pale- or dark-green or yellow vegetable of the squash family. Harvested when young, its edible flowers can be stuffed and deep-fried.

CONVERSION CHART

MEASURES

One Australian metric measuring cup holds approximately 250ml; one Australian metric tablespoon holds 20ml; one Australian metric teaspoon holds 5ml.

The difference between one country's measuring cups and another's is within a two- or three-teaspoon variance, and will not affect your cooking results. North America, New Zealand and the United Kingdom use a 15ml tablespoon.

All cup and spoon measurements are level. The most accurate way of measuring dry ingredients is to weigh them. When measuring liquids, use a clear glass or plastic jug with the metric markings.

The imperial measurements used in these recipes are approximate only. Measurements for cake pans are approximate only. Using same-shaped cake pans of a similar size should not affect the outcome of your baking. We measure the inside top of the cake pan to determine sizes.

We use large eggs with an average weight of 60g.

DRY MEASURES

METRIC	IMPERIAL
15G	½OZ
30G	1OZ
60G	2OZ
90G	3OZ
125G	4OZ (¼LB)
155G	5OZ
185G	6OZ
220G	7OZ
250G	8OZ (½LB)
280G	9OZ
315G	10OZ
345G	11OZ
375G	12OZ (¾LB)
410G	13OZ
440G	14OZ
470G	15OZ
500G	16OZ (1LB)
750G	24OZ (1½LB)
1KG	32OZ (2LB)

LIQUID MEASURES

METRIC	IMPERIAL
30ML	1 FLUID OZ
60ML	2 FLUID OZ
100ML	3 FLUID OZ
125ML	4 FLUID OZ
150ML	5 FLUID OZ
190ML	6 FLUID OZ
250ML	8 FLUID OZ
300ML	10 FLUID OZ
500ML	16 FLUID OZ
600ML	20 FLUID OZ
1000ML (1 LITRE)	1¾ PINTS

LENGTH MEASURES

METRIC	IMPERIAL
3MM	⅛IN
6MM	¼IN
1CM	½IN
2CM	¾IN
2.5CM	1IN
5CM	2IN
6CM	2½IN
8CM	3IN
10CM	4IN
13CM	5IN
15CM	6IN
18CM	7IN
20CM	8IN
22CM	9IN
25CM	10IN
28CM	11IN
30CM	12IN (1FT)

OVEN TEMPERATURES

The oven temperatures in this book are for conventional ovens; if you have a fan-forced oven, decrease the temperature by 10-20 degrees.

	°C (CELSIUS)	°F (FAHRENHEIT)
VERY SLOW	120	250
SLOW	150	300
MODERATELY SLOW	160	325
MODERATE	180	350
MODERATELY HOT	200	400
HOT	220	425
VERY HOT	240	475

INDEX